William John McGee

The Siouan Indians

William John McGee

The Siouan Indians

ISBN/EAN: 9783337305062

Printed in Europe, USA, Canada, Australia, Japan

Cover: Foto ©Andreas Hilbeck / pixelio.de

More available books at **www.hansebooks.com**

THE

SIOUAN INDIANS

A PRELIMINARY SKETCH

BY

W. J. McGEE

EXTRACT FROM THE FIFTEENTH ANNUAL REPORT OF THE
BUREAU OF ETHNOLOGY

WASHINGTON
GOVERNMENT PRINTING OFFICE
1897

CONTENTS

155

THE SIOUAN INDIANS

A PRELIMINARY SKETCH[1]

By W J McGee

THE SIOUAN STOCK

DEFINITION

EXTENT OF THE STOCK

Out of some sixty aboriginal stocks or families found in North America above the Tropic of Cancer, about five-sixths were confined to the tenth of the territory bordering Pacific ocean; the remaining nine-tenths of the land was occupied by a few strong stocks, comprising the Algonquian, Athapascan, Iroquoian, Shoshonean, Siouan, and others of more limited extent.

The Indians of the Siouan stock occupied the central portion of the continent. They were preeminently plains Indians, ranging from Lake Michigan to the Rocky mountains, and from the Arkansas to the Saskatchewan, while an outlying body stretched to the shores of the Atlantic. They were typical American barbarians, headed by hunters and warriors and grouped in shifting tribes led by the chase or driven by battle from place to place over their vast and naturally rich domain, though a crude agriculture sprang up whenever a tribe tarried long in one spot. No native stock is more interesting than the great Siouan group, and none save the Algonquian and Iroquoian approach it in wealth of literary and historical records; for since the advent of white men the Siouan Indians have played striking rôles on the stage of human development, and have caught the eye of every thoughtful observer.

The term *Siouan* is the adjective denoting the "Sioux" Indians and cognate tribes. The word "Sioux" has been variously and vaguely used. Originally it was a corruption of a term expressing enmity or contempt, applied to a part of the plains tribes by the forest dwelling Algonquian Indians. According to Trumbull, it was the popular appellation of those tribes which call themselves Dakota, Lakota, or Nakota

[1] Prepared as a complement and introduction to the following paper on "Siouan Sociology," by the late James Owen Dorsey.

("Friendly," implying confederated or allied , and was an abbreviation of *Nadowessioux*, a Canadian-French corruption of *Nadowe-ssi-wag* ("the snake-like ones" or "enemies"), a term rooted in the Algonquian *nadowe* ("a snake"); and some writers have applied the designation to different portions of the stock, while others have rejected it because of the offensive implication or for other reasons. So long ago as 1836, however, Gallatin employed the term "Sioux" to designate collectively "the nations which speak the Sioux language,"[1] and used an alternative term to designate the subordinate confederacy—i. e., he used the term in a systematic way for the first time to denote an ethnic unit which experience has shown to be well defined. Gallatin's terminology was soon after adopted by Prichard and others, and has been followed by most careful writers on the American Indians. Accordingly the name must be regarded as established through priority and prescription, and has been used in the original sense in various standard publications.[2]

In colloquial usage and in the usage of the ephemeral press, the term "Sioux" was applied sometimes to one but oftener to several of the allied tribes embraced in the first of the principal groups of which the stock is composed, i. e., the group or confederacy styling themselves Dakota. Sometimes the term was employed in its simple form, but as explorers and pioneers gained an inkling of the organization of the group, it was often compounded with the tribal name as "Santee-Sioux," "Yanktonnai-Sioux," "Sisseton Sioux," etc. As acquaintance between white men and red increased, the stock name was gradually displaced by tribe names until the colloquial appellation "Sioux" became but a memory or tradition throughout much of the territory formerly dominated by the great Siouan stock. One of the reasons for the abandonment of the name was undoubtedly its inappropriateness as a designation for the confederacy occupying the plains of the upper Missouri, since it was an alien and opprobrious designation for a people bearing a euphonious appellation of their own. Moreover, colloquial usage was gradually influenced by the usage of scholars, who accepted the native name for the Dakota (spelled Dahcota by Gallatin) confederacy, as well as the tribal names adopted by Gallatin, Prichard, and others. Thus the ill-defined term "Sioux" has dropped out of use in the substantive form, and is retained, in the adjective form only, to designate a great stock to which no other collective name, either intern or alien, has ever been definitely and justly applied.

The earlier students of the Siouan Indians recognized the plains tribes alone as belonging to that stock, and it has only recently been shown that certain of the native forest dwellers long ago encountered by English colonists on the Atlantic coast were closely akin to the

[1] A synopsis of the Indian tribes   in North America   Trans. and Coll. Am. Antiq. Soc., vol. ii, p. 120.

[2] Indian linguistic families of America north of Mexico.   Seventh Annual Report of the Bureau of Ethnology, for 1885-86 (1891), pp. 111-118   Johnson's Cyclopedia 1893-95 edition, vol. vii, p. 546 etc.

plains Indians in language, institutions, and beliefs. In 1872 Hale noted a resemblance between the Tutelo and Dakota languages, and this resemblance was discussed orally and in correspondence with several students of Indian languages, but the probability of direct connection seemed so remote that the affinity was not generally accepted. Even in 1880, after extended comparison with Dakota material (including that collected by the newly instituted Bureau of Ethnology), this distinguished investigator was able to detect only certain general similarities between the Tutelo tongue and the dialects of the Dakota tribes.[1] In 1881 Gatschet made a collection of linguistic material among the Catawba Indians of South Carolina, and was struck with the resemblance of many of the vocables to Siouan terms of like meaning, and began the preparation of a comparative Catawba-Dakota vocabulary. To this the Tutelo, Çegiha, Ḷoiwe're, and Hotcañgara (Winnebago) were added by Dorsey, who made a critical examination of all Catawba material extant and compared it with several Dakota dialects, with which he was specially conversant. These examinations and comparisons demonstrated the affinity between the Dakota and Catawba tongues and showed them to be of common descent; and the establishment of this relation made easy the acceptance of the affinity suggested by Hale between the Dakota and Tutelo.

Up to this time it was supposed that the eastern tribes "were merely offshoots of the Dakota;" but in 1883 Hale observed that "while the language of these eastern tribes is closely allied to that of the western Dakota, it bears evidence of being older in form,"[2] and consequently that the Siouan tribes of the interior seem to have migrated westward from a common fatherland with their eastern brethren bordering the Atlantic. Subsequently Gatschet discovered that the Biloxi Indians of the Gulf coast used many terms common to the Siouan tongues; and in 1891 Dorsey visited these Indians and procured a rich collection of words, phrases, and myths, whereby the Siouan affinity of these Indians was established. Meantime Mooney began researches among the Cherokee and cognate tribes of the southern Atlantic slope and found fresh evidence that their ancient neighbors were related in tongue and belief with the buffalo hunters of the plains; and he has recently set forth the relations of the several Atlantic slope tribes of Siouan affinity in full detail.[3] Through the addition of these eastern tribes the great Siouan stock is augmented in extent and range and enhanced in interest; for the records of a group of cognate tribes are thereby increased so fully as to afford historical perspective and to indicate, if not clearly to display, the course of tribal differentiation.

According to Dorsey, whose acquaintance with the Siouan Indians was especially close, the main portion of the Siouan stock, occupying the continental interior, comprised seven principal divisions (including

[1] Correspondence with the Bureau of Ethnology.
[2] "The Tutelo tribe and language," Proc. Am. Philos. Soc., vol. XXI, 1883, p. 1.
[3] Siouan Tribes of the East; bulletin of the Bureau of Ethnology, 1894.

the Biloxi and not distinguishing the Asiniboin), each composed of one or more tribes or confederacies, all defined and classified by linguistic, social, and mythologic relations; and he and Mooney recognize several additional groups, defined by linguistic affinity or historical evidence of intimate relations, in the eastern part of the country. So far as made out through the latest researches, the grand divisions, confederacies, and tribes of the stock,[1] with their present condition, are as follows:

1. *Dakota-Asiniboin*

Dakota ("Friendly") or Otʻ-ce-ti ca-ko-wiⁿ ("Seven council-fires") confederacy, comprising—

(A) Santee, including Mde-wa-kaⁿ'-toⁿ-waⁿ ("Spirit Lake village") and Wa-qpeʻ-ku te ("Shoot among deciduous trees"), mostly located in Knox county, Nebraska, on the former Santee reservation, with some on Fort Peck reservation, Montana.

(B) Sisseton or Si-siʻ-toⁿ-waⁿ' ("Fish-scale village"), mostly on Sisseton reservation, South Dakota, partly on Devils Lake reservation, North Dakota.

(C) Wahpeton or Waʻ-qpeʻ-toⁿ-waⁿ ("Dwellers among deciduous trees"), mostly on Devils Lake reservation, North Dakota.

(D) Yankton or I-hankʻ-toⁿ-waⁿ ("End village"), in Yankton village, South Dakota.

(E) Yanktonai or I-hankʻ-toⁿ-waⁿ-na ("Little End village"), comprising—

(a) Upper Yanktonai, on Standing Rock reservation, North Dakota, with the Paʻ-ba-kse ("Cut head") gens on Devils Lake reservation, North Dakota.

(b) Lower Yanktonai, or Huñkpatina ("Campers at the horn [or end of the camping circle]"), mostly on Crow Creek reservation, South Dakota, with some on Standing Rock reservation, North Dakota, and others on Fort Peck reservation, Montana.

(F) Teton or Tiʻ-toⁿ-waⁿ ("Prairie dwellers"), comprising—

(a) Brulé or Si-tcaⁿ'-xu ("Burnt thighs"), including Upper Brulé, mostly on Rosebud reservation, South Dakota, and Lower Brulé, on Lower Brulé reservation, in the same state, with some of both on Standing Rock reservation, North Dakota, and others on Fort Peck reservation, Montana.

(b) Sans Arcs or I ta' zip-tco ("Without bows"), largely on Cheyenne reservation, South Dakota, with others on Standing Rock reservation, North Dakota.

(c) Blackfeet or Si ha' sa-pa ("Black-feet"), mostly on Cheyenne reservation, South Dakota, with some on Standing Rock reservation, North Dakota.

---

[1] The subdivisions are set forth in the following treatise on "Siouan Sociology."

(*d*) Minneconjou or Mi'-ni-ko'-o-ju ("Plant beside the stream"), mostly on Cheyenne reservation, South Dakota, partly on Rosebud reservation, South Dakota, with some on Standing Rock reservation, North Dakota.

(*e*) Two Kettles or O-o'-he no"'-pa ("Two boilings"), on Cheyenne reservation, South Dakota.

(*f*) Ogalala or O-gla'-la ("She poured out her own"), mostly on Pine Ridge reservation, South Dakota, with some on Standing Rock reservation, North Dakota, including the Wa-ja'-ja ("Fringed") gens on Pine Ridge reservation, South Dakota, and Loafers or Wa-glu'-xe ("In-breeders"), mostly on Pine Ridge reservation, with some on Rosebud reservation, South Dakota.

(*g*) Huñkpapa ("At the entrance"), on Standing Rock reservation, North Dakota.

Asiniboin ("Cook-with-stones people" in Algonquian), commonly called Nakota among themselves, and called Hohe ("Rebels") by the Dakota; an offshoot from the Yanktonnai; not studied in detail during recent years; partly on Fort Peck reservation, Montana, mostly in Canada; comprising in 1833 (according to Prince Maximilian)[1]—

(*A*) Itscheabiné ("Les gens des filles"=Girl people?).

(*B*) Jatonabiné ("Les gens des roches"=Stone people); apparently the leading band.

(*C*) Otopachgnato ("Les gens du large"=Roamers?).

(*D*) Otaopabiné ("Les gens des canots"=Canoe people?).

(*E*) Tschantoga ("Les gens des bois"=Forest people).

(*F*) Watópachnato ("Les gens de l'age"=Ancient people?).

(*G*) Tanintanei ("Les gens des osayes"=Bone people).

(*H*) Chábin ("Les gens des montagnes"=Mountain people).

2. Çegiha ("People dwelling here")[2]

(*A*) Omaha or U-ma"-ha" ("Upstream people"), located on Omaha reservation, Nebraska, comprising in 1819 (according to James)[3]—

    (*a*) Honga-sha-no tribe, including—

        (1) Wase-ish-ta band.

        (2) Enk-ka-sa-ba band.

---

[1] Travels in the Interior of North America; Translated by H. Evans Lloyd, London, 1843, p. 194. In this and other lists of names taken from early writers the original orthography and interpretation are preserved.

[2] Defined in "The Çegiha Language," by J. Owen Dorsey, Cont. N. A. Eth., vol. VI, 1890, p. xv. Miss Fletcher, who is intimately acquainted with the Omaha, questions whether the relations between the tribes are so close as to warrant the maintenance of this division; yet as an expression of linguistic affinity, at least, the division seems to be useful and desirable.

[3] Account of an Expedition from Pittsburgh to the Rocky Mountains, performed in the Years 1819–1820, under the Command of Major S. H. Long, by Edwin James; London, 1823, vol. II, p. 47 et seq.

(3) Wa-sa-ba-eta-je ("Those who do not touch bears" band.

4 Ka-e-ta-je ("Those who do not touch turtles") band.

5 Wa-jinga-eta-je band.

6) Hun-guh band.

(7) Kon-za band.

8 Ta-pa-taj-je band.

(b) Ish-ta-sun-da ("Gray eyes" tribe, including—

(1) Ta-pa-eta-je band.

(2) Mon-eka-goh ha ("Earth makers") band.

(3 Ta-sin-da "Bison tail") band.

(4 Ing-gera-je-da ("Red dung") band.

(5) Wash-a-tung band.

B) Ponka ("Medicine" ?), mostly on Ponca reservation, Indian Territory, partly at Santee agency, Nebraska.

C) Kwapa, Quapaw, or U-ga'-qpa ("Downstream people," a correlative of U-man'-han), the "Arkansa" of early writers, mostly on Osage reservation, Oklahoma, partly on Quapaw reservation, Indian Territory.

(*D*) Osage or Wa-ca'-ce ("People"), comprising—

(*a*) Big Osage or Pa he'-tsi ("Campers on the mountain"), on Osage reservation, Indian Territory.

(*b*) Little Osage or U-ṣéq'-ta ("Campers on the lowland,") on Osage reservation, Indian Territory.

(*c*) San-ṣu'-ṣḍin¹ ("Campers in the highland grove") or "Arkansa band," chiefly on Osage reservation, Indian Territory.

(*E*) Kansa or Ka″-ze (refers to winds, though precise significance is unknown; frequently called Kaw), on Kansas reservation, Indian Territory.

3. ʟ̣ɪwe'́re (" People of this place")

A Iowa or Pá-qo-tce ("Dusty-heads"), chiefly on Great Nemaha reservation, Kansas and Nebraska, partly on Sac and Fox reservation, Indian Territory.

B) Oto or Wa-to-ta ("Aphrodisian"), on Otoe reservation, Indian Territory.

(*C*) Missouri or Ni-u'-ta-tci (exact meaning uncertain; said to refer to drowning of people in a stream; possibly a corruption of Ni-shu'-dje, "Smoky water," the name of Missouri river); on Otoe reservation, Indian Territory.

4. Winnebago

Winnebago (Algonquian designation, meaning " Turbid water people"? or Ho-tcañ-ga-ra ("People of the parent speech").

¹Corrupted to "Chaucers" in early days. cf James ibid. vol. III, p 10⁸.

mostly on Winnebago reservation in Nebraska, some in Wisconsin, and a few in Michigan; composition never definitely ascertained; comprised in 1850 (according to Schoolcraft[1]) twenty-one bands, all west of the Mississippi, viz.:

(*a*) Little Mills' band.
(*b*) Little Dekonie's band.
(*c*) Maw-kuh-soonch-kaw's band.
(*d*) Ho-pee-kaw's band.
(*e*) Waw-kon-haw-kaw's band.
(*f*) Baptiste's band.
(*g*) Wee-noo-shik's band.
(*h*) Con-a-ha-ta-kaw's band.
(*i*) Paw-sed ech-kaw's band.
(*j*) Taw-nn-nuk's band.
(*k*) Ah-hoo-zeeb-kaw's band.
(*l*) Is-chaw-go-baw-kaw's band.
(*m*) Watch-ha-ta-kaw's band.
(*n*) Waw-maw-noo-kaw-kaw's band.
(*o*) Waw-kon-chaw-zu-kaw's band.
(*p*) Good Thunder's band.
(*q*) Koog-ay-ray-kaw's band.
(*r*) Black Hawk's band.
(*s*) Little Thunder's band.
(*t*) Naw-key-ku-kaw's band.
(*u*) O-chin-chin-nu-kaw's band.

5. *Mandan*

Mandan (their own name is questionable: Catlin says they called themselves See-pohs-kah-nu-mah-kah-kee, " People of the pheasants;"[2] Prince Maximilian says they called themselves Numangkake, "Men," adding usually the name of their village, and that another name is Mahna-Narra, "The Sulky [Ones]," applied because they separated from the rest of their nation;[3] of the latter name their common appellation seems to be a corruption); on Fort Berthold reservation, North Dakota, comprising in 1804 (according to Lewis and Clark[4]) three villages—

(*a*) Matootonha.
(*b*) Rooptahee.
(*c*) ——————— (Eapanopa's village).

[1] Information Respecting the History, Condition, and Prospects of the Indian Tribes of the United States, part 1, Philadelphia, 1853, p. 498.

[2] Letters and Notes on the Manners, Customs, and Condition of the North American Indians, 4th edition: London, 1844, vol. 1, p. 80.

[3] Travels, op. cit , p. 335.

[4] History of the Expedition under the Command of Lewis and Clark, by Elliott Coues, 1893, vol. 1, pp. 182-4. The other two villages enumerated appear to belong rather to the Hidatsa. Prince Maximilian found but two villages in 1833, Mih Tutta Hang-Kush and Ruhptare, evidently corresponding to the first two mentioned by the earlier explorers (op. cit., p. 335).

6. Hidatsa

(A Hidatsa their own name, the meaning of which is uncertain, but appears to refer to a traditional buffalo paunch connected with the division of the group, though supposed by some to refer to "willows"); formerly called Minitari ("Cross the water," or, objectionally, Gros Ventres); on Fort Berthold reservation, North Dakota, comprising in 1796 (according to information gained by Matthews[1]) three villages—

> (a) Hidatsa.
> (b) Amatiha ("Earth-lodge village?"?).
> (c) Amaliami ("Mountain-country [people]"?).

B) Crow or Ab-sa'-ru-ke, on the Crow reservation, Montana.

7. Biloxi

A) Biloxi ("Trifling" or "Worthless" in Choctaw) or Ta-neks' Ha"-ya di' ("Original people" in their own language); partly in Rapides parish, Louisiana; partly in Indian Territory, with the Choctaw and Caddo.

(B) Paskagula ("Bread people" in Choctaw), probably extinct.

(C) ?Moctobi (meaning unknown), extinct.

(D) ?Chozetta (meaning unknown), extinct.

8. Monakan

Monakan confederacy.

> (A Monakan ("Country [people of?]"), ?extinct.
> (B) Meipontsky (meaning unknown), extinct.
> (C) ?Mahoc (meaning unknown), extinct.
> (D) Nuntaneuck or Nuntaly (meaning unknown), extinct.
> (E) Mohetan ("People of the earth"?), extinct.

Tutelo.

> (A) Tutelo or Ye-sa"' (meaning unknown), probably extinct.
> (A') Saponi (meaning unknown), probably extinct. (According to Mooney, the Tutelo and Saponi tribes were intimately connected or identical, and the names were used interchangeably, the former becoming more prominent after the removal of the tribal remnant from the Carolinas to New York.[2])
> B) Occanichi (meaning unknown), probably extinct.

?Manahoac confederacy, extinct.

> (A) Manahoac (meaning unknown).
> (B) Stegarake (meaning unknown).
> (C) Shackakoni (meaning unknown).
> (D) Tauxitania (meaning unknown).

Ethnography and Philology of the Hidatsa Indians, Miscel. Publ. No. 7, U. S. Geol. and Geog. Survey, 1877, p. 38.

[2] Siouan Tribes of the East, p. 37. Local names derived from the Saponi dialect were recognized and interpreted by a Kwapa when pronounced by Dorsey.

(*E*) Outponi (meaning unknown).
(*F*) Tegniati (meaning unknown).
(*G*) Whonkenti (meaning unknown).
(*H*) Hasinninga (meaning unknown).

9. *Catawba or Ni-ya* ("People")

(*A*) Catawba (meaning unknown; they called themselves Ni-ya, "Men" in the comprehensive sense, nearly extinct.
(*B*) Woccon (meaning unknown), extinct.
(*C*) ? Sissipahaw (meaning unknown), extinct.
(*D*) ? Cape Fear (proper name unknown), extinct.
(*E*) ? Warrennuncock (meaning unknown), extinct.
(*F*) ? Adshusheer (meaning unknown), extinct.
(*G*) ? Eno (meaning unknown), extinct.
(*H*) ? Shocco (meaning unknown), extinct.
(*I*) ? Waxhaw (meaning unknown), extinct.
(*J*) ? Sugeri (meaning unknown), extinct.
(*K*) Santee (meaning unknown).
(*L*) Wateree (derived from the Catawba word watéran, "to float in the water").
(*M*) Sewee (meaning unknown).
(*N*) Congaree (meaning unknown).

10. *Sara (extinct)*

(*A*) Sara ("Tall grass").
(*B*) Keyauwi (meaning unknown.

11. *? Pedee (extinct)*

(*A*) Pedee (meaning unknown).
(*B*) Waccamaw (meaning unknown.
(*C*) Winyaw (meaning unknown.
(*D*) "Hooks" and "Backhooks" (?).

The definition of the first six of these divisions is based on extended researches among the tribes and in the literature representing the work of earlier observers, and may be regarded as satisfactory. In some cases, notably the Dakota confederacy, the constitution of the divisions is also satisfactory, though in others, including the Asiniboin, Mandan, and Winnebago, the tabulation represents little more than superficial enumeration of villages and bands, generally by observers possessing little knowledge of Indian sociology or language. So far as the survivors of the Biloxi are concerned the classification is satisfactory; but there is doubt concerning the former limits of the division, and also concerning the relations of the extinct tribes referred to on slender, yet the best available, evidence. The classification of the extinct and nearly extinct Siouan Indians of the east is much less satisfactory. In several cases languages are utterly lost, and in others a few doubtful terms alone remain. In these cases affinity is inferred in part from geographic relation, but chiefly from the recorded federation of tribes and union of remnants as the aboriginal population faded under the light of brighter intelligence; and in all such instances it has been assumed that federation and union grew out of that conformity in mode of thought which is characteristic of peoples speaking identical or closely related tongues. Accordingly, while the grouping of eastern tribes rests in part on meager testimony and is open to question at many points, it is perhaps the best that can be devised, and suffices for convenience of statement if not as a final classification.

So far as practicable the names adopted for the tribes, confederacies, and other groups are those in common use, the aboriginal designations, when distinct, being added in those cases in which they are known.

The present population of the Siouan stock is probably between 40,000 and 45,000, including 2,000 or more (mainly Asiniboin) in Canada.

TRIBAL NOMENCLATURE

In the Siouan stock, as among the American Indians generally, the accepted appellations for tribes and other groups are variously derived. Many of the Siouan tribal names were, like the name of the stock, given by alien peoples, including white men, though most are founded on the descriptive or other designations used in the groups to which they pertain. At first glance, the names seem to be loosely applied and perhaps vaguely defined, and this laxity in application and definition does not disappear, but rather increases, with closer examination.

There are special reasons for the indefiniteness of Indian nomenclature: The aborigines were at the time of discovery, and indeed most of them remain today, in the prescriptorial stage of culture, i. e., the stage in which ideas are crystallized, not by means of arbitrary symbols, but by means of arbitrary associations,[1] and in this stage names are connotive or descriptive, rather than denotive as in the scriptorial stage. Moreover, among the Indians, as among all other prescriptorial peoples, the ego is paramount, and all things are described, much more largely than among cultured peoples, with reference to the describer and the position which he occupies—Self and Here, and, if need be, Now and Thus, are the fundamental elements of primitive conception and description, and these elements are implied and exemplified, rather than expressed, in thought and utterance. Accordingly there is a notable paucity in names, especially for themselves, among the Indian tribes, while the descriptive designations applied to a given group by neighboring tribes are often diverse.

[1] The leading culture stages are defined in the Thirteenth Annual Report of the Bureau of Ethnology, for 1891–92 (1896), p. xxiii et seq.

The principles controlling nomenclature in its inchoate stages are illustrated among the Siouan peoples. So far as their own tongues were concerned, the stock was nameless, and could not be designated save through integral parts. Even the great Dakota confederacy, one of the most extensive and powerful aboriginal organizations, bore no better designation than a term probably applied originally to associated tribes in a descriptive way and perhaps used as a greeting or countersign, although there was an alternative proper descriptive term—"Seven Council fires"—apparently of considerable antiquity, since it seems to have been originally applied before the separation of the Asiniboin.[1] In like manner the Çegiha, Ḷoiwe're, and Hoteañgara groups, and perhaps the Ṇiya, were without denotive designations for themselves, merely styling themselves "Local People," "Men," "Inhabitants," or, still more ambitiously, "People of the Parent Speech," in terms which are variously rendered by different interpreters; they were lords in their own domain, and felt no need for special title. Different Dakota tribes went so far as to claim that their respective habitats marked the middle of the world, so that each insisted on precedence as the leading tribe,[2] and it was the boast of the Mandan that they were the original people of the earth.[3] In the more carefully studied confederacies the constituent groups generally bore designations apparently used for convenient distinction in the confederation; sometimes they were purely descriptive, as in the case of the Sisseton, Wahpeton, Sans Arcs, Blackfeet, Oto, and several others; again they referred to the federate organization (probably, possibly to relative position of habitat), as in the Yankton, Yanktonai, and Huñkpapa; more frequently they referred to geographic or topographic position, e. g., Teton, Omaha, Pahe'tsi, Kwapa, etc; while some appear to have had a figurative or symbolic connotation, as Brulé, Ogalala, and Ponka. Usually the designations employed by alien peoples were more definite than those used in the group designated, as illustrated by the stock name, Asiniboin, and Iowa. Commonly the alien appellations were terms of reproach; thus Sioux, Biloxi, and Hohe (the Dakota designation for the Asiniboin) are clearly opprobrious, while Paskagula might easily be opprobrious among hunters and warriors, and Iowa and Oto appear to be derogatory or contemptuous expressions. The names applied by the whites were sometimes taken from geographic positions, as in the case of Upper Yanktonai and Cape Fear—the geographic names themselves being frequently of Indian origin. Some of the current names represent translations of the aboriginal terms either into English ("Blackfeet," "Two Kettles," "Crow,") or into French ("Sans Arcs," "Brulé," "Gros Ventres"); yet most of the names, at least of the prairie tribes, are simply corruptions of the aboriginal terms, though frequently the modification is so complete as to render identification and interpretation difficult—it

[1] Cf. Schoolcraft, "Information," etc, op. cit., pt. ii, 1852, p. 169. Dorsey was inclined to consider the number as made up without the Asiniboin.

[2] Riggs-Dorsey: "Dakota Grammar, Texts, and Ethnography," Cont. N. A. Eth., vol. ix, 1893, p. 164

[3] Catlin: "Letters and Notes," op. cit., p. 80.

is not easy to find Waca'ce in "Osage" (so spelled by the French, whose orthography was adopted and mispronounced by English-speaking pioneers , or Pa'qotce in " Iowa."

The meanings of most of the eastern names are lost; yet so far as they are preserved they are of a kind with those of the interior. So, too, are the subtribal names enumerated by Dorsey.

PRINCIPAL CHARACTERS

PHONETIC AND GRAPHIC ARTS

The Siouan stock is defined by linguistic characters. The several tribes and larger and smaller groups speak dialects so closely related as to imply occasional or habitual association, and hence to indicate community in interests and affinity in development; and while the arts (reflecting as they did the varying environment of a wide territorial range) were diversified, the similarity in language was, as is usual, accompanied by similarity in institutions and beliefs. Nearly all of the known dialects are eminently vocalic, and the tongues of the plains, which have been most extensively studied, are notably melodious; thus the leading languages of the group display moderately high phonetic development. In grammatic structure the better-known dialects are not so well developed; the structure is complex, chiefly through the large use of inflection, though agglutination sometimes occurs. In some cases the germ of organization is found in fairly definite juxtaposition or placement. The vocabulary is moderately rich, and of course represents the daily needs of a primitive people, their surroundings, their avocations, and their thoughts, while expressing little of the richer ideation of cultured cosmopolites. On the whole, the speech of the Siouan stock may be said to have been fairly developed, and may, with the Algonquian, Iroquoian, and Shoshonean, be regarded as typical for the portion of North America lying north of Mexico. Fortunately it has been extensively studied by Riggs, Hale, Dorsey, and several others, including distinguished representatives of some of the tribes, and is thus accessible to students. The high phonetic development of the Siouan tongues reflects the needs and records the history of the hunter and warrior tribes, whose phonetic symbols were necessarily so differentiated as to be intelligible in whisper, oratory, and war cry, as well as in ordinary converse, while the complex structure is in harmony with the elaborate social organization and ritual of the Siouan people.

Many of the Siouan Indians were adepts in the sign language; indeed, this mode of conveying intelligence attained perhaps its highest development among some of the tribes of this stock, who, with other plains Indians, developed pantomime and gesture into a surprisingly perfect art of expression adapted to the needs of huntsmen and warriors.

Most of the tribes were fairly proficient in pictography; totemic and other designs were inscribed on bark and wood, painted on skins, wrought into domestic wares, and sometimes carved on rocks. Jonathan Carver gives an example of picture-writing on a tree, in charcoal mixed with bear's grease, designed to convey information from the "Chipe'ways" (Algonquian to the "Naudowessies," and other instances of intertribal communication by means of pictography are on record. Personal decoration was common, and was largely symbolic; the face and body were painted in distinctive ways when going on the warpath, in organizing the hunt, in mourning the dead, in celebrating the victory, and in performing various ceremonials. Scarification and maiming were practiced by some of the tribes, always in a symbolic way. Among the Mandan and Hidatsa scars were produced in cruel ceremonials originally connected with war and hunting, and served as enduring witnesses of courage and fortitude. Symbolic tattooing was fairly common among the westernmost tribes. Eagle and other feathers were worn as insignia of rank and for other symbolic purposes, while bear claws and the scalps of enemies were worn as symbols of the chase and battle. Some of the tribes recorded current history by means of "winter counts" or calendaric inscriptions, though their arithmetic was meager and crude, and their calendar proper was limited to recognition of the year, lunation, and day—or, as among so many primitive people, the "snow," "dead moon," and "night,"—with no definite system of fitting lunations to the annual seasons. Most of the graphic records were perishable, and have long ago disappeared; but during recent decades several untutored tribesmen have executed vigorous drawings representing hunting scenes and conflicts with white soldiery, which have been preserved or reproduced. These crude essays in graphic art were the germ of writing, and indicate that, at the time of discovery, several Siouan tribes were near the gateway opening into the broader field of scriptorial culture. So far as it extends, the crude graphic symbolism betokens warlike habit and militant organization, which were doubtless measurably inimical to further progress.

It would appear that, in connection with their proficiency in gesture speech and their meager graphic art, the Siouan Indians had become masters in a vaguely understood system of dramaturgy or symbolized conduct. Among them the use of the peace-pipe was general; among several and perhaps all of the tribes the definite use of insignia was common; among them the customary hierarchic organization of the aborigines was remarkably developed and was maintained by an elaborate and strict code of etiquette whose observance was exacted and yielded by every tribesman. Thus the warriors, habituated to expressing and recognizing tribal affiliation and status in address and deportment, were notably observant of social minutiae, and this habit extended into every activity of their lives. They were ceremonious among themselves and

[Travels Through the Interior Parts of North America in the Years 1766, 1767, and 1768; London, 1778, p. 418.

crafty toward enemies, tactful diplomatists as well as brave soldiers, shrewd strategists as well as fierce fighters; ever they were skillful readers of human nature, even when ruthless takers of human life. Among some of the tribes every movement and gesture and expression of the male adult seems to have been affected or controlled with the view of impressing spectators and auditors, and through constant schooling the warriors became most consummate actors. To the casual observer, they were stoics or stupids according to the conditions of observation; to many observers, they were cheats or charlatans; to scientific students, their eccentrically developed volition and the thaumaturgy by which it was normally accompanied suggests early stages in that curious development which, in the Orient, culminates in necromancy and occultism. Unfortunately this phase of the Indian character (which was shared by various tribes was little appreciated by the early travelers, and little record of it remains; yet there is enough to indicate the importance of constantly studied ceremony, or symbolic conduct, among them. The development of affectation and self-control among the Siouan tribesmen was undoubtedly shaped by warlike disposition, and their stoicism was displayed largely in war—as when the captured warrior went exultingly to the torture, taunting and tempting his captors to multiply their atrocities even until his tongue was torn from its roots, in order that his fortitude might be proved; but the habit was firmly fixed and found constant expression in commonplace as well as in more dramatic actions.

INDUSTRIAL AND ESTHETIC ARTS

Since the arts of primitive people reflect environmental conditions with close fidelity, and since the Siouan Indians were distributed over a vast territory varying in climate, hydrography, geology, fauna, and flora, their industrial and esthetic arts can hardly be regarded as distinctive, and were indeed shared by other tribes of all neighboring stocks.

The best developed industries were hunting and warfare, though all of the tribes subsisted in part on fruits, nuts, berries, tubers, grains, and other vegetal products, largely wild, though sometimes planted and even cultivated in rude fashion. The southwestern tribes, and to some extent all of the prairie denizens and probably the eastern remnant, grew maize, beans, pumpkins, melons, squashes, sunflowers, and tobacco, though their agriculture seems always to have been subordinated to the chase. Aboriginally, they appear to have had no domestic animals except dogs, which, according to Carver—one of the first white men seen by the prairie tribes,—were kept for their flesh, which was eaten ceremonially,[1] and for use in the chase.[2] According to

---

[1] Op. cit., p. 278.

[2] Op. cit., p. 445. Carver says: "The dogs employed by the Indians in hunting appear to be all of the same species they carry their ears erect, and greatly resemble a wolf about the head. They are exceedingly useful to them in their hunting excursions and will attack the fiercest of the game they are in pursuit of. They are also remarkable for their fidelity to their masters, but being ill fed by them are very troublesome in their huts or tents."

Lewis and Clark (1804–1806), they were used for burden and draft;[1] according to the naturalists accompanying Long's expedition (1819–20), for flesh (eaten ceremonially and on ordinary occasions), draft, burden, and the chase,[2] and according to Prince Maximilian, for food and draft,[3] all these functions indicating long familiarity with the canines. Catlin, too, found "dog's meat . . . the most honorable food that can be presented to a stranger;" it was eaten ceremonially and on important occasions.[4] Moreover, the terms used for the dog and his harness are ancient and even archaic, and some of the most important ceremonials were connected with this animal,[5] implying long-continued association. Casual references indicate that some of the tribes lived in mutual tolerance with several birds[6] and mammals not yet domesticated (indeed the buffalo may be said to have been in this condition), so that the people were at the threshold of zooculture.

The chief implements and weapons were of stone, wood, bone, horn, and antler. According to Carver, the "Nadowessie" were skillful bowmen, using also the "casse-tête"[7] or warclub, and a flint scalping-knife. Catlin was impressed with the shortness of the bows used by the prairie tribes, though among the southwestern tribes they were longer. Many of the Siouan Indians used the lance, javelin, or spear. The domestic utensils were scant and simple, as became wanderers and fighters, wood being the common material, though crude pottery

[1] Coues, "History of the Expedition," op. cit., vol. 1, p. 140. A note adds, "The dogs are not large, much resemble a wolf, and will haul about 70 pounds each."

[2] Narrative of an Expedition to the Source of St. Peter's River . . . under the Command of Stephen H. Long, U. S. T. E., by William H. Keating; London, 1825, vol. 1. p. 451; vol. 11, p. 44, et al. Account of an Expedition from Pittsburgh to the Rocky Mountains . . . under the Command of Major S. H. Long, U. S. T E., by Edwin James; London, 1823, vol. 1, pp. 155, 182, et al.

Say remarks (James, loc. cit., p. 155) of the coyote (?), "This animal . . . is probably the original of the domestic dog, so common in the villages of the Indians of this region [about Council Bluffs and Omaha], some of the varieties of which still retain much of the habit and manners of this species." James says (loc. cit., vol. 11, p. 13), "The dogs of the Konzas are generally of a mixed breed, between our dogs with pendent ears and the native dogs, whose ears are universally erect. The Indians of this nation seek every opportunity to cross the breed. These mongrel dogs are less common with the Omawhaws, while the dogs of the Pawnees generally have preserved their original form."

[3] Travels in the Interior of North America; London, 1843. The Prince adds, "In shape they differ very little from the wolf, and are equally large and strong. Some are of the real wolf color; others are black, white, or spotted with black and white, and differing only by the tail being rather more turned up. Their voice is not a proper barking, but a howl like that of the wolf, and they partly descend from wolves, which approach the Indian huts, even in the daytime and mix with the dogs" (cf. p. 203 et al.). Writing at the Mandan village, he says, "The Mandans and Manitaries have not, by any means, so many dogs as the Assiniboin, Crows, and Blackfeet. They are rarely of true wolf color, but generally black or white, or else resemble the wolf, but here they are more like the prairie wolf (Canis latrans). We likewise found among these animals a brown race, descended from European pointers; hence the genuine bark of the dog is more frequently heard here, whereas among the western nations they only howl. The Indian dogs are worked very hard, have hard blows and hard fare; in fact, they are treated just as this fine animal is treated among the Esquimaux" (p. 345).

[4] "Letters and Notes," etc, vol. 1, p. 14; cf. p. 230 et al. He speaks (p. 201) of the Minitari canines as "semiloup dogs and whelps."

[5] Keating's "Narrative," op. cit., vol. 11, p. 452; James' "Account," op. cit., vol. 1, p. 127 et al.

[6] According to Prince Maximilian, both the Mandan and Minitari kept owls in their lodges and regarded them as soothsayers ("Travels," op. cit., pp. 383, 400), and the eagle was apparently tolerated for the sake of his feathers.

[7] "Cassa Tate, the antient tomahawk" on the plate illustrating the objects ("Travels," op. cit., pl. 4, p. 298).

and basketry were manufactured, together with bags and bottles of skins or animal intestines. Ceremonial objects were common, the most conspicuous being the calumet, carved out of the sacred pipestone or catlinite quarried for many generations in the midst of the Siouan territory. Frequently the pipes were fashioned in the form of tomahawks, when they carried a double symbolic significance, standing alike for peace and war, and thus expressing well the dominant idea of the Siouan mind. Tobacco and kinnikinic (a mixture of tobacco with shredded bark, leaves, etc⁴) were smoked.

Aboriginally the Siouan apparel was scanty, commonly comprising breechclout, moccasins, leggings, and robe, and consisted chiefly of dressed skins, though several of the tribes made simple fabrics of bast, rushes, and other vegetal substances. Fur robes and rush mats commonly served for bedding, some of the tribes using rude bedsteads. The buffalo hunting prairie tribes depended largely for apparel, bedding, and habitations, as well as for food, on the great beast to whose comings and goings their movements were adjusted. Like other Indians, the Siouan hunters and their consorts quickly availed themselves of the white man's stuffs, as well as his metal implements, and the primitive dress was soon modified.

The woodland habitations were chiefly tent-shape structures of saplings covered with bark, rush mats, skins, or bushes; the prairie habitations were mainly earth lodges for winter and buffalo-skin tipis for summer. Among many of the tribes these domiciles, simple as they were, were constructed in accordance with an elaborate plan controlled by ritual. According to Morgan, the framework of the aboriginal Dakota house consisted of 13 poles;² and Dorsey describes the systematic grouping of the tipis belonging to different gentes and tribes. Sudatories were characteristic in most of the tribes, menstrual lodges were common, and most of the more sedentary tribes had council houses or other communal structures. The Siouan domiciles were thus adapted with remarkable closeness to the daily habits and environment of the tribesmen, while at the same time they reflected the complex social organization growing out of their prescriptorial status and militant disposition.

Most of the Siouan men, women, and children were fine swimmers, though they did not compare well with neighboring tribes as makers and managers of water craft. The Dakota women made coracles of buffalo hides, in which they transported themselves and their householdry, but the use of these and other craft seems to have been regarded as little better than a feminine weakness. Other tribes were better boatmen; for the Siouan Indian generally preferred land travel to journeying by water, and avoided the burden of vehicles by which his

¹ Described by Cones, "History of the Expedition under the Command of Lewis and Clark," 1893, vol. I, p. 159, note.
² "Houses and House-life of the American Aborigines," Cont. N. A. Eth., vol. IV, 1881, p. 114.

ever-varying movements in pursuit of game or in waylaying and evading enemies would have been limited and handicapped.

There are many indications and some suggestive evidences that the chief arts and certain institutions and beliefs, as well as the geographic distribution, of the principal Siouan tribes were determined by a single conspicuous feature in their environment—the buffalo. As Riggs, Hale, and Dorsey have demonstrated, the original home of the Siouan stock lay on the eastern slope of the Appalachian mountains, stretching down over the Piedmont and Coastplain provinces to the shores of the Atlantic between the Potomac and the Savannah. As shown by Allen, the buffalo, "prior to the year 1800," spread eastward across the Appalachians[1] and into the priscan territory of the Siouan tribes. As suggested by Shaler, the presence of this ponderous and peaceful animal materially affected the vocations of the Indians, tending to discourage agriculture and encourage the chase; and it can hardly be doubted that the bison was the bridge that carried the ancestors of the western tribes from the crest of the Alleghenies to the Côteau des Prairies and enabled them to disperse so widely over the plains beyond. Certainly the toothsome flesh and useful skins must have attracted the valiant huntsmen among the Appalachians; certainly the feral herds must have become constantly larger and more numerous westward, thus tempting the pursuers down the waterways toward the great river; certainly the vast herds beyond the Mississippi gave stronger incentives and richer rewards than the hunters of big game found elsewhere; and certainly when the prairie tribes were discovered, the men and animals lived in constant interaction, and many of the hunters acted and thought only as they were moved by their easy prey. As the Spanish horse spread northward over the Llano Estacado and overflowed across the mountains from the plains of the Cayuse, the Dakota and other tribes found a new means of conquest over the herds, and entered on a career so facile that they increased and multiplied despite strife and imported disease.

The horse was acquired by the prairie tribes toward the end of the last century. Carver (1766–1768) describes the methods of hunting among the "Naudowessie" without referring to the horse,[2] though he gives their name for the animal in his vocabulary,[3] and describes their mode of warfare with "Indians that inhabit still farther to the westward a country which extends to the South Sea," having "great plenty of horses."[4] Lewis and Clark (1804–1806) mention that the "Sioux of the Teton tribe . . . frequently make excursions to steal horses" from the Mandan,[5] and make other references indicating that the horse

[1] "The American Bisons, Living and Extinct," by J. A. Allen; Memoirs of the Geol. Survey of Kentucky, vol. i, pt. ii, 1876, map; also pp. 55, 72–101, et al.

[2] Op. cit., p. 283 et seq.

[3] Ibid., p. 435.

[4] Ibid., p. 294.

[5] "History of the Expedition under the Command of Lewis and Clark," etc, by Elliott Coues, 1893 vol. i, p. 175. It is noted that in winter the Mandan kept their horses in their lodges at night, and fed them on cottonwood branches. Ibid., pp. 220, 233, et al.

was in fairly common use among some of the Siouan tribes, though the animal was "confined principally to the nations inhabiting the great plains of the Columbia," and dogs were still used for burden and draft. Grinnell learned from an aged Indian that horses came into the hands of the neighboring Piegan (Algonquian) about 1804–1806. Long's naturalists found the horse, ass, and mule in use among the Kansa and other tribes, and described the mode of capture of wild horses by the Osage; yet when, two-thirds of a century after Carver, Catlin (1832–1839) and Prince Maximilian (1833–34) visited the Siouan territory, they found the horse established and in common use in the chase and in war. It is significant that the Dakota word for horse (šuṅ-taṅ'-ka or šuṅ-ka'-wa-kaṅ) is composed of the word for dog (šuṅ'-ka', with an affix indicating greatness, sacredness, or mystery, so that the horse is literally "great mysterious dog," or "ancient sacred dog," and that several terms for harness and other appurtenances correspond with those used for the gear of the dog when used as a draft animal. This terminology corroborates the direct evidence that the dog was domesticated by the Siouan aborigines long before the advent of the horse.

Among the Siouan tribes, as among other Indians, amusements absorbed a considerable part of the time and energy of the old and young of both sexes. Among the young, the gambols, races, and other sports were chiefly or wholly diversional, and commonly mimicked the avocations of the adults. The girls played at the building and care of houses and were absorbed in dolls, while the boys played at archery, foot racing, and mimic hunting, which soon grew into the actual chase of small birds and animals. Some of the sports of the elders were unorganized diversions, leaping, racing, wrestling, and other spontaneous expressions of exuberance. Certain diversions were controlled by more persistent motive, as when the idle warrior occupied his leisure in meaningless ornamentation of his garment or tipi, or spent hours of leisure in esthetic modification of his weapon or ceremonial badge, and to this purposeless activity, which engendered design with its own progress, the incipient graphic art of the tribes was largely due. The more important and characteristic sports were organized and interwoven with social organization and belief so as commonly to take the form of elaborate ceremonial, in which dancing, feasting, fasting, symbolic painting, song, and sacrifice played important parts, and these organized sports were largely fiducial. To many

¹ Cones, Expedition of Lewis and Clark, vol. III, p. 839.
² Ibid., vol. I, p. 140.
  "The Story of the Indian," 1895, p. 237.
⁴ James "Account," op. cit., vol. I, pp. 126, 148; vol. II, p. 12 et al.
⁵ Ibid., vol. III, p. 107.
⁶ "Letters and Notes," op. cit., vol. I, pp. 142 (where the manner of lassoing wild horses is mentioned) p. 251 et al.; "Travels," op. cit., p. 149 et al. (The Crow were said to have between 9,000 and 10,000 head, p. 174.)
⁷ Keating in Long's Expedition, op. cit., vol. II, appendix, p. 152. Riggs' "Dakota-English Dictionary," Cont. N. A. Eth., vol. VII, 1890.

of the early observers the observances were nothing more than meaningless mummeries; to some they were sacrilegious, to others sortilegious; to the more careful students, like Carver, whose notes are of especial value by reason of the author's clear insight into the Indian character, they were invocations, expiations, propitiations, expressing profound and overpowering devotion. Carver says of the "Naudowessie." "They usually dance either before or after every meal; and by this cheerfulness, probably, render the Great Spirit, to whom they consider themselves as indebted for every good, a more acceptable sacrifice than a formal and unanimated thanksgiving;"[1] and he proceeds to describe the informal dances as well as the more formal ceremonials preparatory to joining in the chase or setting out on the warpath. The ceremonial observances of the Siouan tribes were not different in kind from those of neighboring contemporaries, yet some of them were developed in remarkable degree—for example, the bloody rites by which youths were raised to the rank of warriors in some of the prairie tribes were without parallel in severity among the aborigines of America, or even among the known primitive peoples of the world. So the sports of the Siouan Indians were both diversional and divinatory, and the latter were highly organized in a manner reflecting the environment of the tribes, their culture-status, their belief, and especially their disposition toward bloodshed; for their most characteristic ceremonials were connected, genetically if not immediately, with warfare and the chase.

Among many of the Siouan tribes, games of chance were played habitually and with great avidity, both men and women becoming so absorbed as to forget avocations and food, mothers even neglecting their children; for, as among other primitive peoples, the charm of hazard was greater than among the enlightened. The games were not specially distinctive, and were less widely differentiated than in certain other Indian stocks. The sport or game of chungke stood high in favor among the young men in many of the tribes, and was played as a game partly of chance, partly of skill; but dice games (played with plum stones among the southwestern prairie tribes) were generally preferred, especially by the women, children, and older men. The games were partly, sometimes wholly, diversional, but generally they were in large part divinatory, and thus reflected the hazardous occupations and low culture-status of the people. One of the evils resulting from the advent of the whites was the introduction of new games of chance which tended further to pervert the simple Siouan mind; but in time the evil brought its own remedy, for association with white gamblers taught the ingenuous sortilegers that there is nothing divine or sacred about the gaming table or the conduct of its votaries.

The primitive Siouan music was limited to the chant and rather simple vocal melody, accompanied by rattle, drum, and flute, the drum among the northwestern tribes being a skin bottle or bag of water.

[1] Op. cit., p. 265.

The music of the Omaha and some other tribes has been most appreciatively studied by Miss Fletcher, and her memoir ranks among the Indian classics. In general the Siouan music was typical for the aboriginal stocks of the northern interior. Its dominant feature was rhythm, by which the dance was controlled, though melody was inchoate, while harmony was not yet developed.

The germ of painting was revealed in the calendars and the seed of sculpture in the carvings of the Siouan Indians. The pictographic paintings comprised not only recognizable but even vigorous representations of men and animals, depicted in form and color though without perspective, while the calumet of catlinite was sometimes chiseled into striking verisimilitude of human and animal forms in miniature. To the collector these representations suggest fairly developed art, though to the Indian they were mainly, if not wholly, symbolic; for everything indicates that the primitive artisan had not yet broken the shackles of fetichistic symbolism, and had little conception of artistic portrayal for its own sake.

INSTITUTIONS

Among civilized peoples, institutions are crystallized in statutes about nuclei of common law or custom; among peoples in the prescriptorial culture-stage statutes are unborn, and various mnemonic devices are employed for fixing and perpetuating institutions; and, as is usual in this stage, the devices involve associations which appear to be essentially arbitrary at the outset, though they tend to become natural through the survival of the fittest. A favorite device for perpetuating institutions among the primitive peoples of many districts on different continents is the taboo, or prohibition, which is commonly fiducial but is often of general application. This device finds its best development in the earlier stages in the development of belief, and is normally connected with totemism. Another device, which is remarkably widespread, as shown by Morgan, is kinship nomenclature. This device rests on a natural and easily ascertained basis, though its applications are arbitrary and vary widely from tribe to tribe and from culture-status to culture-status. A third device, which found much favor among the American aborigines and among some other primitive peoples, may be called *ordination*, or the arrangement of individuals and groups classified from the prescriptorial point of view of Self, Here, and Now, with respect to each other or to some dominant personage or group. This device seems to have grown out of the kin name system, in which the Ego is the basis from which relation is reckoned. It tends to develop into federate organization on the one hand or into caste on the other hand, according to the attendant conditions.[2] There are various other

[1] A study of Omaha Indian Music by Alice C. Fletcher . . . aided by Francis La Flesche, with a report on the structural peculiarities of the music, by John Comfort Fillmore, A. M.; Arch. and Eth. papers of the Peabody Museum, vol. 1, No. 5, 1893; pp. i-vi 7-152 (231)-252.

[2] Ordination, as the term is here used, comprehends regimentation as defined by Powell, yet relates especially to the method of reckoning from the constantly recognized but ever varying standpoint of prescriptorial culture.

devices for fixing and perpetuating institutions or for expressing the laws embodied therein.   Some of these are connected with thaumaturgy and shamanism, some are connected with the powers of nature, and the several devices overlap and interlace in puzzling fashion.

Among the Siouan Indians the devices of taboo, kin-names, and ordination are found in such relation as to throw some light on the growth of primitive institutions.   While they blend and are measurably involved with thaumaturgic devices, there are indications that in a general way the three devices stand for stages in the development of law.   Among the best-known tribes the taboo pertained to the clan, and was used (in a much more limited way than among some other peoples) to commemorate and perpetuate the clan organization; kin-names, which were partly natural and thus normal to the clan organization, and at the same time partly artificial and thus characteristic of gentile organization, served to commemorate and perpetuate not only the family relations but the relations of the constituent elements of the tribe; while the ordination expressed in the camping circle, in the phratries, in the ceremonials, and in many other ways, served to commemorate intertribal as well as intergentile relations, and thus to promote peace and harmonious action.   It is significant that the taboo was less potent among the Siouan Indians than among some other stocks, and that among some tribes it has not been found; and it is especially significant that in some instances the taboo was apparently inversely related to kin-naming and ordination, as among the Biloxi, where the taboo is exceptionally weak and kin-naming exceptionally strong, and among the Dakota, where the system of ordination attained perhaps its highest American development in domiciliary arrangement, while the taboo was limited in function; for the relations indicate that the taboo was archaic or even vestigial.   It is noteworthy also that among most of the Siouan tribes the kin-name system was less elaborate than in many other stocks, while the system of ordination is so elaborate as to constitute one of the leading characteristics of the stock.

At the time of the discovery, most of the Siouan tribes had apparently passed into gentile organization, though vestiges of clan organization were found—e. g., among the best-known tribes the man was the head of the family, though the tipi usually belonged to the woman.   Thus, as defined by institutions, the stock was just above savagery and just within the lower stages of barbarism.   Accordingly the governmental functions were hereditary in the male line, yet the law of heredity was subject to modification or suspension at the will of the group, commonly at the instance of rebels or usurpers of marked prowess or shrewdness. The property regulations were definite and strictly observed; as among other barbarous peoples, the land was common to the tribe or other group occupying it, yet was defended against alien invasion; the ownership of movable property was a combination of communalism and individualism delicately adjusted to the needs and habits of the several tribes—

in general, evanescent property, such as food and fuel, was shared in common—subject to carefully regulated individual claims—, while permanent property, such as tipis, dogs, apparel, weapons, etc, was held by individuals. As among other tribes, the more strictly personal property was usually destroyed on the death of the owner, though the real reason for the custom—the prevention of dispute—was shrouded in a mantle of mysticism.

Although of primary importance in shaping the career of the Siouan tribes, the marital institutions of the stock were not specially distinctive. Marriage was usually effected by negotiation through parents or elders; among some of the tribes the bride was purchased, while among others there was an interchange of presents. Polygyny was common; in several of the tribes the bride's sisters became subordinate wives of the husband. The regulations concerning divorce and the punishment of infidelity were somewhat variable among the different tribes, some of whom furnished temporary wives to distinguished visitors. Generally there were sanctions for marriage by elopement or individual choice. In every tribe, so far as known, gentile exogamy prevailed—i. e., marriage in the gens was forbidden, under pain of ostracism or still heavier penalty, while the gentes intermarried among one another; in some cases intermarriage between certain tribes was regarded with special favor. There seems to have been no system of marriage by capture, though captive women were usually espoused by the successful tribesmen, and girls were sometimes abducted. In general it would appear that intergentile and intertribal marriage was practiced and sanctioned by the sages, and that it tended toward harmony and federation, and thus contributed much toward the increase and diffusion of the great Siouan stock.

As set forth in some detail by Dorsey, the ordination of the Siouan tribes extended beyond the hierarchic organization into families, subgentes, gentes, tribes, and confederacies; there were also phratries, sometimes (perhaps typically) arranged in pairs; there were societies or associations established on social or fiducial bases; there was a general arrangement or classification of each group on a military basis, as into soldiers and two or more classes of noncombatants, etc. Among the Siouan peoples, too, the individual brotherhood of the David-Jonathan or Damon-Pythias type was characteristically developed. Thus the corporate institutions were interwoven and superimposed in a manner nearly as complex as that found in the national, state, municipal, and minor institutions of civilization; yet the ordination preserved by means of the camping circle, the kinship system, the simple series of taboos, and the elaborate symbolism was apparently so complete as to meet every social and governmental demand.

BELIEFS

THE DEVELOPMENT OF MYTHOLOGY

As explained by Powell, philosophies and beliefs may be seriated in four stages: The first stage is hecastotheism; in this stage extranatural or mysterious potencies are imputed to objects both animate

and inanimate. The second stage is zootheism; within it the powers
of animate forms are exaggerated and amplified into the realm of the
supernal, and certain animals are deified. The third stage is that of
physitheism, in which the agencies of nature are personified and
exalted unto omnipotence. The fourth stage is that of psychotheism,
which includes the domain of spiritual concept. In general the development of belief coincides with the growth of abstraction; yet it is to
be remembered that this growth represents increase in definiteness of
the abstract concepts rather than augmentation in numbers and kinds
of subjective impressions, i. e., the advance is in quality rather than
in quantity; indeed, it would almost appear that the vague and indefinite abstraction of hecastotheism is more pervasive and prevalent than
the clearer abstraction of higher stages. Appreciation of the fundamental characteristics of belief is essential to even the most general
understanding of the Indian mythology and philosophy, and even after
careful study it is difficult for thinkers trained in the higher methods
of thought to understand the crude and confused ideation of the
primitive thinker.

In hecastotheism the believer finds mysterious properties and potencies everywhere. To his mind every object is endued with occult
power, moved by a vague volition, actuated by shadowy motive ranging capriciously from malevolence to benevolence; in his lax estima-
tion some objects are more potent or more mysterious than others, the
strong, the sharp, the hard, and the swift-moving rising superior to
the feeble, the dull, the soft, and the slow. Commonly he singles out
some special object as his personal, family, or tribal mystery-symbol
or fetich, the object usually representing that which is most feared or
worst hated among his surroundings. Vaguely realizing from the
memory of accidents or unforeseen events that he is dependent on his
surroundings, he invests every feature of his environment with a
capricious humor reflecting his own disposition, and gives to each and
all a subtlety and inscrutability corresponding to his exalted estima-
tion of his own craft in the chase and war; and, conceiving himself to
live and move only at the mercy of his multitudinous associates, he
becomes a fatalist—kismet is his watchword, and he meets defeat and
death with resignation, just as he goes to victory with complacence;
for so it was ordained.

Zootheism is the offspring of hecastotheism. As the primitive
believer assigns special potency or mystery to the strong and the swift,
he gradually comes to give exceptional rank to self-moving animals;
as his experience of the strength, alertness, swiftness, and courage of
his animate enemy or prey increases, these animals are invested with
successively higher and higher attributes, each reflecting the mental
operations of the mystical huntsman, and in time the animals with
which the primitive believers are most intimately associated come to be
regarded as tutelary daimons of supernatural power and intelligence.
At first the animals, like the undifferentiated things of hecastotheism,

are regarded in fear or awe by reason of their strength and ferocity, and this regard grows into an incipient worship in the form of sacrifice or other ceremonial; meanwhile, inanimate things, and in due season rare and unimportant animals, are neglected, and a half dozen, a dozen, or a score of the well-known animals are exalted into a hierarchy of petty gods, headed by the strongest like the bear, the swiftest like the deer, the most majestic like the eagle, the most cunning like the fox or coyote, or the most deadly like the rattlesnake. Commonly the arts and the skill of the mystical huntsman improve from youth to adolescence and from generation to generation, so that the later animals appear to be easier snared or slain than the earlier; moreover, the accounts of conflicts between men and animals grow by repetition and are gilded by imagination as memory grows dim; and for these and other reasons the notion grows up that the ancient animals were stronger, swifter, slier, statelier, deadlier than their modern representatives, and the hierarchy of petty gods is exalted into an omnipotent thearchy. Eventually, in the most highly developed zootheistic systems, the leading beast-god is regarded as the creator of the lesser deities of the earth, sun, and sky, of the mythic under-world and its real counterpart the ground or mid-world, as well as the visionary upper-world, of men, and of the ignoble animals; sometimes the most exalted beast-god is worshiped especially by the great man or leading class and incidentally by all, while other men and groups choose the lesser beast-gods, according to their rank, for special worship. In hecastotheism the potencies revered or worshiped are polymorphic, while their attributes reflect the mental operations of the believers; in zootheism the deities worshiped are zoomorphic, and their attributes continue to reflect the human mind.

Physitheism, in its turn, springs from zootheism. Through contemplation of the strong the idea of strength arises, and a means is found for bringing the bear into analogy with thunder, with the sun, or with the avalanche-bearing mountain; through contemplation of the swift the concept of swiftness is engendered, and comparison of the deer with the wind or rushing river is made easy; through contemplation of the deadly stroke of the rattlesnake the notion of death-dealing power assumes shape, and comparison of the snake bite and the lightning stroke is made possible; and in every case it is inevitably perceived that the agency is stronger, swifter, deadlier than the animal. At first the agency is not abstracted or dissociated from the parent zootheistic concept, and the sun is the mightiest animal as among many peoples, the thunder is the voice of the bear as among different woodland tribes or the flapping of the wings of the great ancient eagle as among the Dakota and Ȼegiha, while lightning is the great serpent of the sky as among the Zuñi. Subsequently the zoic concept fades, and the constant association of human intellectual qualities engenders an anthropic concept, when the sun becomes an anthropomorphic deity (perhaps bearing a dazzling mask, as among the Zuñi), and thunder is the rumbling of quoits pitched by the shades of old-time giants, as among different American tribes. Eventually all the leading agencies of nature are personified in anthropic form, and retain the human attributes of caprice, love, and hate which are found in the minds of the believers.

Psychotheism is born of physitheism as the anthropomorphic element in the concept of natural agency gradually fades; but since none of the aborigines of the United States had passed into the higher stage, the mode of transition does not require consideration.

It is to be borne in mind that throughout the course of development of belief, from the beginning of hecastotheism into the borderland of psychotheism, the dominant characteristic is the vague notion of mystery. At first the mystery pervades all things and extends in all directions, representing an indefinite ideal world, which is the counterpart of the real world with the addition of human qualities. Gradually the mystery segregates, deepening with respect to animals and disappearing with respect to inanimate things; and at length the slowly changing mysteries shape themselves into semiabstractions having a strong anthropic cast, while the remainder of the earth and the things thereof gradually become real, though they remain under the spell and dominion of the mysterious. Thus at every stage the primitive believer is a mystic—a fatalist in one stage, a beast worshiper in another, a thaumaturgist in a third, yet ever and first of all a mystic. It is also to be borne in mind (and the more firmly because of a widespread misapprehension) that the primitive believer, up to the highest stage attained by the North American Indian, is not a psychotheist, much less a monotheist. His "Great Spirit" is simply a great mystery, perhaps vaguely anthropomorphic, oftener zoomorphic, yet not a spirit, which he is unable to conceive save by reflection of the white man's concept and inquiry; and his departed spirit is but a shade, much like that of the ancient Greeks, the associate and often the inferior of animal shades.

While the four stages in development of belief are fundamentally distinct, they nevertheless overlap in such manner as apparently, and in a measure really, to coexist and blend. Culture progress is slow. In biotic development the effect of beneficial modification is felt immediately, and the modified organs or organisms are stimulated and strengthened cumulatively, while the unmodified are enfeebled and paralyzed cumulatively through inactivity and quickly pass toward atrophy and extinction. Conversely in demotic development, which is characterized by the persistence of the organisms and by the elimination of the bad and the preservation of the good among qualities only, there is a constant tendency toward retardation of progress; for in savagery and barbarism as in civilization, age commonly produces conservatism, and at the same time brings responsibility for the conduct of old and young, so that modification, howsoever beneficial, is

measurably held in check, and so that the progress of each generation
buds in the springtime of youth yet is not permitted to fruit until the
winter of old age approaches. Accordingly the mean of demotic progress tends to lag far behind its foremost advances, and modes of
action and especially of thought change slowly. This is especially true
of beliefs, which, during each generation, are largely vestigial. So the
stages in the evolution of mythologic philosophy overlap widely; there
is probably no tribe now living among whom zootheism has not yet
taken root, though hecastotheism has been found dominant among
different tribes; there is probably no people in the zootheistic stage
who are completely divested of hecastotheistic vestiges; and one of the
curious features of even the most advanced psychotheism is the occasional outcropping of features inherited from all of the earlier stages.
Yet it is none the less important to discriminate the stages.

THE SIOUAN MYTHOLOGY

It was partly through pioneer study of the Siouan Indians that the
popular fallacy concerning the aboriginal "Great Spirit" gained cur-
rency; and it was partly through the work of Dorsey among the Ǫegiha
and Dakota tribes, first as a missionary and afterward as a linguist,
that the early error was corrected. Among these tribes the creation
and control of the world and the things thereof are ascribed to
"wakaⁿda" (the term varying somewhat from tribe to tribe), just as
among the Algonquian tribes omnipotence was assigned to "ma-ni-do"
("Manito the Mighty" of "Hiawatha"); yet inquiry shows that
wakaⁿda assumes various forms, and is rather a quality than a definite
entity. Thus, among many of the tribes the sun is wakaⁿda—not *the*
wakaⁿda or *a* wakaⁿda, but simply wakaⁿda; and among the same
tribes the moon is wakaⁿda, and so is thunder, lightning, the stars, the
winds, the cedar, and various other things; even a man, especially a
shaman, might be wakaⁿda or a wakaⁿda. In addition the term was
applied to mythic monsters of the earth, air, and waters; according to
some of the sages the ground or earth, the mythic under-world, the
ideal upper-world, darkness, etc, were wakaⁿda or wakaⁿdas. So, too,
the fetiches and the ceremonial objects and decorations were wakaⁿda
among different tribes. Among some of the groups various animals
and other trees besides the specially wakaⁿda cedar were regarded as
wakaⁿdas; as already noted, the horse, among the prairie tribes, was
the wakaⁿda dog. In like manner many natural objects and places of
striking character were considered wakaⁿda. Thus the term was
applied to all sorts of entities and ideas, and was used (with or without inflectional variations) indiscriminately as substantive and adjective, and with slight modification as verb and adverb. Manifestly a
term so protean is not susceptible of translation into the more highly
differentiated language of civilization. Manifestly, too, the idea
expressed by the term is indefinite, and can not justly be rendered into
"spirit," much less into "Great Spirit;" though it is easy to under-

stand how the superficial inquirer, dominated by definite spiritual concept, handicapped by unfamiliarity with the Indian tongue, misled by ignorance of the vague prescriptorial ideation, and perhaps deceived by crafty native informants or mischievous interpreters, came to adopt and perpetuate the erroneous interpretation. The term may be translated into "mystery" perhaps more satisfactorily than into any other single English word, yet this rendering is at the same time much too limited and much too definite. As used by the Siouan Indian, wakaⁿda vaguely connotes also "power," "sacred," "ancient," "grandeur," "animate," "immortal," and other words, yet does not express with any degree of fullness and clearness the ideas conveyed by these terms singly or collectively—indeed, no English sentence of reasonable length can do justice to the aboriginal idea expressed by the term wakaⁿda.

While the beliefs of many of the Siouan tribes are lost through the extinction of the tribesmen or transformed through acculturation, it is fortunate that a large body of information concerning the myths and ceremonials of several prairie tribes has been collected. The records of Carver, Lewis and Clark, Say, Catlin, and Prince Maximilian are of great value when interpreted in the light of modern knowledge. More recent researches by Miss Fletcher[1] and by Dorsey[2] are of especial value, not only as direct sources of information but as a means of interpreting the earlier writings. From these records it appears that, in so far as they grasped the theistic concept, the Siouan Indians were polytheists; that their mysteries or deities varied in rank and power; that some were good but more were bad, while others combined bad and good attributes; that they assumed various forms, actual and imaginary; and that their dispositions and motives resembled those found among mankind.

The organization of the vague Siouan thearchy appears to have varied from group to group. Among all of the tribes whose beliefs are known, the sun was an important wakaⁿda, perhaps the leading one potentially, though usually of less immediate consideration than certain others, such as thunder, lightning, and the cedar tree; among the Osage the sun was invoked as "grandfather," and among various tribes there were sun ceremonials, some of which are still maintained; among the Omaha and Ponka, according to Miss Fletcher, the mythic thunder bird plays a prominent, perhaps dominant rôle, and the cedar tree or pole is deified as its tangible representative. The moon was wakaⁿda among the Osage and the stars among the Omaha and Ponka, yet they seem to have occupied subordinate positions; the winds and the four quarters were apparently given higher rank; and, in individual cases, the mythic water-monsters or earth-deities seem to have occupied leading positions. On the whole, it may be safe to consider the

[1] Several of these are summarized in "The emblematic use of the tree in the Dakota group," Science, n. s., vol. iv, 1896, pp. 475–487.
[2] Notably "A Study of Siouan Cults," Seventh Annual Report of the Bureau of Ethnology for 1889–90 (1894), pp. 351–544.

sun as the Siouan arch-mystery, with the mythic thunder-bird or
family of thunder birds as a sort of mediate link between the mysteries
and men, possessing less power but displaying more activity in human
affairs than the remoter waka"da of the heavens. Under these controlling waka"das, other members of the series were vaguely and variably
arranged. Somewhere in the lower ranks, sacred animals—especially
sports, such as the white buffalo cow—were placed, and still lower
came totems and shamans, which, according to Dorsey, were reverenced
rather than worshiped. It is noteworthy that this thearchic arrangement corresponded in many respects with the hierarchic social organization of the stock.

The Siouan thearchy was invoked and adored by means of forms
and ceremonies, as well as through orisons. The set observances were
highly elaborate; they comprised dancing and chanting, feasting and
fasting, and in some cases sacrifice and torture, the shocking atrocities
of the Mandan and Minitari rites being especially impressive. From
these great collective devotions the ceremonials graded down through
war dance and hunting-feast to the terpsichorean grace extolled by
Carver, and to individual fetich worship. In general the adoration
expressed fear of the evil rather than love of the good—but this can
hardly be regarded as a distinctive feature, much less a peculiar one.

Some of the mystery places were especially distinctive and noteworthy. Foremost among them was the sacred pipestone quarry near
Big Sioux river, whence the material for the waka"da calumet was
obtained; another was the far-famed Minne-waka" of North Dakota,
not inaptly translated "Devil's lake;" a third was the mystery-rock or
medicine-rock of the Mandan and Hidatsa near Yellowstone river; and
there were many others of less importance. About all of these places
picturesque legends and myths clustered.

The Siouan mythology is especially instructive, partly because so
well recorded, partly because it so clearly reflects the habits and
customs of the tribesmen and thus gives an indirect reflection of a
well-marked environment. As among so many peoples, the sun is a
prominent element; the ice-monsters of the north and the rain-myths
of the arid region are lacking, and are replaced by the frequent thunder and the trees shaken by the storm-winds; the mythic creatures are
shaped in the image of the indigenous animals and birds; the myths
center in the local rocks and waters; the mysterious thearchy corre-
sponds with the tribal hierarchy, and the attributes ascribed to the
deities are those characteristic of warriors and hunters.

Considering the mythology in relation to the stages in development
of mythologic philosophy, it appears that the dominant beliefs, such as
those pertaining to the sun and the winds, represent a crude physitheism, while vestiges of hecastotheism crop out in the object-worship
and place-worship of the leading tribes and in other features. At the

same time well-marked zootheistic features are found in the mythic thunder-birds and in the more or less complete deification of various animals, in the exaltation of the horse into the rank of the mythic dog father, and in the animal forms of the water-monsters and earth beings; and the living application of zootheism is found in the animal fetiches and totems. On the whole, it seems just to assign the Siouan mythology to the upper strata of zootheism, just verging on physitheism, with vestigial traces of hecastotheism.

SOMATOLOGY

The vigorous avocations of the chase and war were reflected in fine stature, broad and deep chests, strong and clean limbs, and sound constitution among the Siouan tribesmen and their consorts. The skin was of the usual coppery cast characteristic of the native American; the teeth were strong, indicating and befitting a largely carnivorous diet, little worn by sandy foods, and seldom mutilated; the hands and feet were commonly large and sinewy. The Siouan Indians were among those who impressed white pioneers by the parallel placing of the feet; for, as among other walkers and runners, who rest sitting and lying, the feet assumed the pedestrian attitude of approximate parallelism rather than the standing attitude of divergence forward. The hair was luxuriant, stiff, straight, and more uniformly jet black than that of the southerly stocks; it was worn long by the women and most of the men, though partly clipped or shaved in some tribes by the warriors as well as the worthless dandies, who, according to Catlin, spent more time over their toilets than ever did the grande dame of Paris. The women were beardless and the men more or less nearly so; commonly the men plucked out by the roots the scanty hair springing on their faces, as did both sexes that on other parts of the body. The crania were seldom deformed artificially save through cradle accident, and while varying considerably in capacity and in the ratio of length to width were usually mesocephalic. The facial features were strong, yet in no way distinctly unlike those found among neighboring peoples.

Since the advent of white men the characteristics of the Siouan Indians, like those of other tribes, have been somewhat modified, partly through infusion of Caucasian blood but chiefly through acculturation. With the abandonment of hunting and war and the tardy adoption of a slothful, semidependent agriculture, the frame has lost something of its stalwart vigor; with the adaptation of the white man's costume and the incomplete assimilation of his hygiene, various weaknesses and disorders have been developed; and through imitation the erstwhile luxuriant hair is cropped, and the beard, made scanty through generations of extirpation, is commonly cultivated. Although the acultural condition of the Siouan survivors ranges from the essentially primitive status of the Asiniboin to the practical civilization of the representatives of several tribes, it is fair to consider the stock in a state of transition from barbarism to civilization; and many of the tribesmen are losing the characteristics of activity and somatic development normal to primitive life, while they have not yet assimilated the activities and acquired the somatic characteristics normal to peaceful sedentary life.

Briefly, certain somatic features of the Siouan Indians, past and present, may be traced to their causes in custom and exercise of function; yet by far the greater number of the features are common to the American people or to all mankind, and are of ill-understood significance. The few features of known cause indicate that special somatic characteristics are determined largely or wholly by industrial and other arts, which are primarily shaped by environment.

HABITAT

Excepting the Asiniboin, who are chiefly in Canada, nearly all of the Siouan Indians are now gathered on the reservations indicated on earlier pages, most of these reservations lying within the aboriginal territory of the stock.

At the advent of white men, the Siouan territory was vaguely defined, and its limits were found to vary somewhat from exploration to exploration. This vagueness and variability of habitat grew out of the characteristics of the tribesmen. Of all the great stocks south of the Arctic, the Siouan was perhaps least given to agriculture, most influenced by hunting, and most addicted to warfare; thus most of the tribes were but feebly attached to the soil, and freely followed the movements of the feral fauna as it shifted with climatic vicissitudes or was driven from place to place by excessive hunting or by fires set to destroy the undergrowth in the interests of the chase; at the same time, the borderward tribes were alternately driven and led back and forth through strife against the tribes of neighboring stocks. Accordingly the Siouan habitat can be outlined only in approximate and somewhat arbitrary fashion.

The difficulty in defining the priscan home of the Siouan tribes is increased by its vast extent and scant peopling, by the length of the period intervening between discovery in the east and complete exploration in the west, and by the internal changes and migrations which occurred during this period. The task of collating the records of exploration and pioneer observation concerning the Siouan and other stocks was undertaken by Powell a few years ago, and was found to be of great magnitude. It was at length successfully accomplished, and the respective areas occupied by the several stocks were approximately mapped.[1]

As shown on Powell's map, the chief part of the Siouan area comprised a single body covering most of the region of the Great plains.

[1] Seventh Annual Report of the Bureau of Ethnology for 1885-86 (1891), pp. 1-142, and map.

stretching from the Rocky mountains to the Mississippi and from the
Arkansas-Red river divide nearly to the Saskatchewan, with an arm
crossing the Mississippi and extending to Lake Michigan. In addition
there were a few outlying bodies, the largest and easternmost bordering
the Atlantic from Santee river nearly to Capes Lookout and Hatteras,
and skirting the Appalachian range northward to the Potomac; the
next considerable area lay on the Gulf coast about Pascagoula river
and bay, stretching nearly from the Pearl to the Mobile; and there were
one or two unimportant areas on Ohio river, which were temporarily
occupied by small groups of Siouan Indians during recent times.

There is little probability that the Siouan habitat, as thus outlined,
ran far into the prehistoric age. As already noted, the Siouan Indians
of the plains were undoubtedly descended from the Siouan tribes of the
east (indeed the Mandan had a tradition to that effect); and reason has
been given for supposing that the ancestors of the prairie hunters followed the straggling buffalo through the cis-Mississippi forests into
his normal trans-Mississippi habitat and spread over his domain save
as they were held in check by alien huntsmen, chiefly of the warlike
Caddoan and Kiowan tribes; and the buffalo itself was a geologically
recent—indeed essentially post-glacial—animal. Little if any definite
trace of Siouan occupancy has been found in the more ancient prehistoric works of the Mississippi valley. On the whole it appears probable
that the prehistoric development of the Siouan stock and habitat was
exceptionally rapid, that the Siouan Indians were a vigorous and virile
people that arose quickly under the stimulus of strong vitality (the
acquisition of which need not here be considered), coupled with exceptionally favorable opportunity, to a power and glory culminating about
the time of discovery.

ORGANIZATION

The demotic organization of the Siouan peoples, so far as known, is
set forth in considerable detail in Mr Dorsey's treatises[1] and in the
foregoing enumeration of tribes, confederacies, and other linguistic
groups.

Like the other aborigines north of Mexico, the Siouan Indians were
organized on the basis of kinship, and were thus in the stage of tribal
society. All of the best-known tribes had reached that plane in organization characterized by descent in the male line, though many vestiges
and some relatively unimportant examples of descent in the female line
have been discovered. Thus the clan system was obsolescent and the
gentile system fairly developed; i. e., the people were practically out
of the stage of savagery and well advanced in the stage of barbarism.

---

[1]Chiefly "Omaha Sociology," Third Ann. Rep. Bur. Eth. for 1881-82 (1884), pp. 205-370, "A study of
Siouan cults," Eleventh Ann. Rep. Bur. Eth., for 1889-90 (1894), pp. 351-544, and that printed on the
following pages.

Confederation for defense and offense was fairly defined and was strengthened by intermarriage between tribes and gentes and the prohibition of marriage within the gens; yet the organization was such as to maintain tribal autonomy in considerable degree; i. e., the social structure was such as to facilitate union in time of war and division into small groups adapted to hunting in times of peace. No indication of feudalism has been found in the stock.

The government was autocratic, largely by military leaders sometimes (particularly in peace) advised by the elders and priests; the leadership was determined primarily by ability—prowess in war and the chase and wisdom in the council,—and was thus hereditary only a little further than characteristics were inherited; indeed, excepting slight recognition of the divinity that doth hedge about a king, the leaders were practically self chosen, arising gradually to the level determined by their abilities. The germ of theocracy was fairly developed, and apparently burgeoned vigorously during each period of peace, only to be checked and withered during the ensuing war when the shamans and their craft were forced into the background.

During recent years, since the tribes began to yield to the domination of the peace-loving whites, the government and election are determined chiefly by kinship, as appears from Dorsey's researches; yet definite traces of the militant organization appear, and any man can win name and rank in his gens, tribe, or confederacy by bravery or generosity.

The institutional connection between the Siouan tribes of the plains and those of the Atlantic slope and the Gulf coast is completely lost, and it is doubtful whether the several branches have ever been united in a single confederation (or "nation," in the language of the pioneers), at least since the division in the Appalachian region perhaps five or ten centuries ago. Since this division the tribes have separated widely, and some of the bloodiest wars of the region in the historic period have been between Siouan tribes; the most extensive union possessing the slightest claim to federal organization was the great Dakota confederacy, which was grown into instability and partial disruption; and most of the tribal unions and coalitions were of temporary character.

Although highly elaborate (perhaps because of this character), the Siouan organization was highly unstable; with every shock of conflict, whether intestine or external, some autocrats were displaced or slain; and after each important event—great battle, epidemic, emigration, or destructive flood—new combinations were formed. The undoubtedly rapid development of the stock, especially after the passage of the Mississippi, indicates growth by conquest and assimilation as well as by direct propagation (it is known that the Dakota and perhaps other groups adopted aliens regularly); and, doubtless for this reason in part, there was a strong tendency toward differentiation and dichotomy in the demotic growth. In some groups the history is too vague to indicate this tendency with certainty; in others the tendency is clear.

Perhaps the best example is found in the Çegiha, which divided into two great branches, the stronger of which threw off minor branches in the Osage and Kansa, and afterward separated into the Omaha and Ponka, while the feebler branch also ramified widely; and only less notable is the example of the Winnebago trunk, with its three great branches in the Iowa, Oto, and Missouri. This strong divergent tendency in itself suggests rapid, perhaps abnormally rapid, growth in the stock; for it outran and partially concealed the tendency toward convergence and ultimate coalescence which characterizes demotic phenomena.

The half-dozen eastern stocks occupying by far the greater part of North America contrast strongly with the half-hundred local stocks covering the Pacific coast; and none of the strong Atlantic stocks is more characteristic, more sharply contrasted with the limited groups of the western coast, or better understood as regards organization and development, than the great Siouan stock of the northern interior. There is promise that, as the demology of aboriginal America is pushed forward, the records relating to the Siouan Indians and especially to their structure and institutions will aid in explaining why some stocks are limited and others extensive, why large stocks in general characterize the interior and small stocks the coasts, and why the dominant peoples of the fifteenth and sixteenth centuries were successful in displacing the preexistent and probably more primitive peoples of the Mississippi valley. While the time is not yet ripe for making final answer to these inquiries, it is not premature to suggest a relation between a peculiar development of the aboriginal stocks and a peculiar geographic conformation: In general the coastward stocks are small, indicating a provincial shoreland habit, yet their population and area commonly increase toward those shores indented by deep bays, along which maritime and inland industries naturally blend; so (confining attention to eastern United States) the extensive Muskhogean stock stretches inland from the deep-bayed eastern Gulf coast; and so, too, three of the largest stocks on the continent (Algonquian, Iroquoian, Siouan) stretch far into the interior from the still more deeply indented Atlantic coast. In two of these cases (Iroquoian and Siouan) history and tradition indicate expansion and migration from the land of bays between Cape Lookout and Cape May, while in the third there are similar (though perhaps less definite) indications of an inland drift from the northern Atlantic bays and along the Laurentian river and lakes.

HISTORY[1]

DAKOTA-ASINIBOIN

The Dakota are mentioned in the Jesuit Relations as early as 1639–40; the tradition is noted that the Ojibwa, on arriving at the Great Lakes in an early migration from the Atlantic coast, encountered representatives

---

[1] Taken chiefly from notes and manuscripts prepared by Mr Dorsey.

of the great confederacy of the plains. In 1641 the French voyageurs
met the Potawatomi Indians flying from a nation called Nadawessi
(enemies ; and the Frenchmen adopted the alien name for the warlike
prairie tribes. By 1658 the Jesuits had learned of the existence of
thirty Dakota villages west northwest from the Potawatomi mission St
Michel; and in 1689 they recorded the presence of tribes apparently
representing the Dakota confederacy on the upper Mississippi, near
the mouth of the St Croix. According to Croghan's History of Western
Pennsylvania, the "Sue" Indians occupied the country southwest of
Lake Superior about 1759; and Dr T. S. Williamson, "the father of the
Dakota mission," states that the Dakota must have resided about the
confluence of the Mississippi and the Minnesota or St Peters for at
least two hundred years prior to 1860.

According to traditions collected by Dorsey, the Teton took posses-
sion of the Black Hills region, which had previously been occupied by
the Crow Indians, long before white men came; and the Yankton
and Yanktonnai, which were found on the Missouri by Lewis and Clark,
were not long removed from the region about Minnesota river. In 1862
the Santee and other Dakota tribes united in a formidable outbreak
in which more than 1,000 whites were massacred or slain in battle.
Through this outbreak and the consequent governmental action toward
the control and settlement of the tribes, much was learned concerning
the characteristics of the people, and various Indian leaders became
known; Spotted Tail, Red Cloud, Crazy Horse, Sitting Bull, American
Horse, and Even-his-horse-is-feared (commonly miscalled Man-afraid-of-
his-horses) were among the famous Dakota chiefs and warriors, notable representatives of a passing race, whose names are prominent in
the history of the country. Other outbreaks occurred, the last of note
resulting from the ghost-dance fantasy in 1890-91, which fortunately
was quickly suppressed. Yet, with slight interruptions, the Dakota
tribes in the United States were steadily gathered on reservations.
Some 800 or more still roam the prairies north of the international
boundary, but the great body of the confederacy, numbering nearly
28,000, are domiciled on reservations (already noted) in Minnesota,
Montana, Nebraska, North Dakota, and South Dakota.

The separation of the Asiniboin from the Wazi-kute gens of the
Yanktonai apparently occurred before the middle of the seventeenth
century, since the Jesuit relation of 1658 distinguishes between the
Ponalak or Guerriers (undoubtedly the Dakota proper) and the Assini-
ponalak or Guerriers de pierre. The Asiniboin are undoubtedly the
Essanape (Essanapi or Assinapi) who were next to the Makatapi
(Dakota) in the Walam-Olum record of the Lenni-Lenape or Delaware.
In 1680 Hennepin located the Asniiboin northeast of the Issati (Isan-
yati or Santee) who were on Knife lake (Minnesota); and the Jesuit
map of 1681 placed them on Lake-of-the-Woods, then called "L. Assi-
neponalaes." La Hontan claimed to have visited the Eokoro (Arikara)

in 1689–90, when the Essanape were sixty leagues above; and Perrot's Mémoire refers to the Asiniboin as a Sioux tribe which, in the seventeenth century, seceded from their nation and took refuge among the rocks of Lake-of-the-Woods. Chauvignerie located some of the tribe south of Ounipigan (Winnipeg) lake in 1736, and they were near Lake-of-the-Woods as late as 1766, when they were said to have 1,500 warriors. It is well known that in 1829 they occupied a considerable territory west of the Dakota and north of Missouri river, with a population estimated at 8,000; and Drake estimated their number at 10,000 before the smallpox epidemic of 1838, which is said to have carried off 4,000. From this blow the tribe seems never to have fully recovered, and now numbers probably no more than 3,000, mostly in Canada, where they continue to roam the plains they have occupied for half a century.

ÇEGIHA

According to tribal traditions collected by Dorsey, the ancestors of the Omaha, Ponka, Kwapa, Osage, and Kansa were originally one people dwelling on Ohio and Wabash rivers, but gradually working westward. The first separation took place at the mouth of the Ohio, when those who went down the Mississippi became the Kwapa or Downstream People, while those who ascended the great river became the Omaha or Up-stream People. This separation must have occurred at least as early as 1500, since it preceded De Soto's discovery of the Mississippi.

The Omaha group (from whom the Osage, Kansa, and Ponka were not yet separated) ascended the Mississippi to the mouth of the Missouri, where they remained for some time, though war and hunting parties explored the country northwestward, and the body of the tribe gradually followed these pioneers, though the Osage and Kansa were successively left behind. Some of the pioneer parties discovered the pipestone quarry, and many traditions cling about this landmark. Subsequently they were driven across the Big Sioux by the Yankton Indians, who then lived toward the confluence of the Minnesota and Mississippi. The group gradually differentiated and finally divided through the separation of the Ponka, probably about the middle of the seventeenth century. The Omaha gathered south of the Missouri, between the mouths of the Platte and Niobrara, while the Ponka pushed into the Black Hills country.

The Omaha tribe remained within the great bend of the Missouri, opposite the mouth of the Big Sioux, until white men came. Their hunting ground extended westward and southwestward, chiefly north of the Platte and along the Elkhorn, to the territory of the Ponka and the Pawnee (Caddoan); and in 1766 Carver met their hunting parties on Minnesota river. Toward the end of the eighteenth century they were nearly destroyed by smallpox, their number having been reduced from about 3,500 to but little over 300 when they were visited by Lewis and Clark, their famous chief Blackbird being one of those carried off by the epidemic. Subsequently they increased in numbers; in 1890 their population was about 1,200. They are now on reservations, mostly owning land in severalty, and are citizens of the United States and of the state of Nebraska.

Although the name Ponka did not appear in history before 1700 it must have been used for many generations earlier, since it is an archaic designation connected with the social organization of several tribes and the secret societies of the Osage and Kansa, as well as the Ponka. In 1700 the Ponka were indicated on De l'Isle's map, though they were not then segregated territorially from the Omaha. They, too, suffered terribly from the smallpox epidemic, and when met by Lewis and Clark in 1804 numbered only about 200. They increased rapidly, reaching about 600 in 1829 and some 800 in 1842; in 1871, when they were first visited by Dorsey, they numbered 747. Up to this time the Ponka and Dakota were amicable; but a dispute grew out of the cession of lands, and the Teton made annual raids on the Ponka until the enforced removal of the tribe to Indian Territory took place in 1877. Through this warfare, more than a quarter of the Ponka lost their lives. The displacement of this tribe from lands owned by them in fee simple attracted attention, and a commission was appointed by President Hayes in 1880 to inquire into the matter; the commission, consisting of Generals Crook and Miles and Messrs William Stickney and Walter Allen, visited the Ponka settlements in Indian Territory and on the Niobrara and effected a satisfactory arrangement of the affairs of the tribe, through which the greater portion (some 600) remained in Indian Territory, while some 225 kept their reservation in Nebraska.

When the Çegiha divided at the mouth of the Ohio, the ancestors of the Osage and Kansa accompanied the main Omaha body up the Mississippi to the mouth of Osage river. There the Osage separated from the group, ascending the river which bears their name. They were distinguished by Marquette in 1673 as the "Ouchage" and "Autrechaha," and by Penicaut in 1719 as the "Huzzau," "Ous," and "Wawha." According to Croghan, they were, in 1759, on "White creek, a branch of the Mississippi," with the "Grand Tue;" but "White creek" (or White water) was an old designation for Osage river, and "Grand Tue" is, according to Mooney, a corruption of "Grandes Eaux," or Great Osage; and there is accordingly no sufficient reason for supposing that they returned to the Mississippi. Toward the close of the eighteenth century the Osage and Kansa encountered the Comanche and perhaps other Shoshonean peoples, and their course was turned southward; and in 1817, according to Brown, the Great Osage and Little Osage were chiefly on Osage and Arkansas rivers, in four villages. In 1829 Porter described their country as beginning 25 miles west of the Missouri line and running to the Mexican line of that date, being 50 miles wide; and he gave their number as 5,000. According to

Schoolcraft, they numbered 3,758 in April, 1853, but this was after the removal of an important branch known as Black Dog's band to a new locality farther down Verdigris river. In 1850 the Osage occupied at least seven large villages, besides numerous small ones, on Neosho and Verdigris rivers. In 1873, when visited by Dorsey, they were gathered on their reservations in what is now Oklahoma. In 1890 they numbered 158.

The Kansa remained with the Up stream People in their gradual ascent of the Missouri to the mouth of the Kaw or Kansas, when they diverged westward; but they soon came in contact with inimical peoples, and, like the Osage, were driven southward. The date of this divergence is not fixed, but it must have been after 1723, when Bourgmont mentioned a large village of "Quans" located on a small river flowing northward thirty leagues above Kaw river, near the Missouri. After the cession of Louisiana to the United States, a treaty was made with the Kansa Indians, who were then on Kaw river, at the mouth of the Saline, having been forced back from the Missouri by the Dakota; they then numbered about 1,500 and occupied about thirty earth lodges. In 1825 they ceded their lands on the Missouri to the Government, retaining a reservation on the Kaw, where they were constantly subjected to attacks from the Pawnee and other tribes, through which large numbers of their warriors were slain. In 1846 they again ceded their lands and received a new reservation on Neosho river in Kansas. This was soon overrun by settlers, when another reservation was assigned to them in Indian Territory, near the Osage country. By 1890 their population was reduced to 214.

The Kwapa were found by De Soto in 1541 on the Mississippi above the mouth of the St Francis, and, according to Marquette's map, they were partly east of the Mississippi in 1673. In 1681 La Salle found them in three villages distributed along the Mississippi, and soon afterward Tonty mentioned four villages, one (Kappa=Uqaqpaqti, "Real Kwapa") on the Mississippi and three (Toyengan=Ta"wa"jiqa, "Small Village"; Toriman=Ti nadéiman, and Osotonoy=Uzutiuwe) inland; this observation was verified by Dorsey in 1883 by the discovery that these names are still in use. In early days the Kwapa were known as "Akansa," or Arkansa, first noted by La Metairie in 1682. It is probable that this name was an Algonquian designation given because of confusion with, or recognition of affinity to, the Kansa or Ka"ze, the prefix "a" being a common one in Algonquian appellations. In 1687 Jontel located two of the villages of the tribe on the Arkansas and two on the Mississippi, one of the latter being on the eastern side. According to St Cosme, the greater part of the tribe died of smallpox in October, 1699. In 1700 De l'Isle placed the principal "Acansa" village on the southern side of Arkansas river; and, according to Gravier, there were in 1701 five villages, the largest, Imaha (Omaha), being highest on the Arkansas. In 1805 Sibley placed the "Arkensa" in three villages on the southern side of Arkansas river, about 12 miles above Arkansas post. They claimed to be the original proprietors of the country bordering the Arkansas for 300 miles, or up to the confluence of the Cadwa, above which lay the territory of the Osage. Subsequently the Kwapa affiliated with the Caddo Indians, though of another stock; according to Porter they were in the Caddo country in 1829. As reservations were established, the Kwapa were re-segregated, and in 1877 were on their reservation in northwestern Indian Territory; but most of them afterward scattered, chiefly to the Osage country, where in 1890 they were found to number 232.

ḶᴏIWEʹRE

The ancestry and prehistoric movements of the tribes constituting this group are involved in considerable obscurity, though it is known from tradition as well as linguistic affinity that they sprung from the Winnebago.

Since the days of Marquette (1673) the Iowa have ranged over the country between the Mississippi and Missouri, up to the latitude of Oneota (formerly upper Iowa) river, and even across the Missouri about the mouth of the Platte. Chauvignerie located them in 1736 west of the Mississippi and (probably through error in identification of the waterway) south of the Missouri; and in 1761 Jefferys placed them between Missouri river and the headwaters of Des Moines river, above the Oto and below the Maha (Omaha). In 1805, according to Drake, they dwelt on Des Moines river, forty leagues above its mouth, and numbered 800. In 1811 Pike found them in two villages on Des Moines and Iowa rivers. In 1815 they were decimated by smallpox, and also lost heavily through war against the tribes of the Dakota confederacy. In 1829 Porter placed them on the Little Platte, some 15 miles from the Missouri line, and about 1853 Schoolcraft located them on Nemaha river, their principal village being near the mouth of the Great Nemaha. In 1848 they suffered another epidemic of smallpox, by which 100 warriors, besides women and children, were carried off. As the country settled, the Iowa, like the other Indians of the stock, were collected on reservations which they still occupy in Kansas and Oklahoma. According to the last census their population was 273.

The Missouri were first seen by Tonty about 1670; they were located near the Mississippi on Marquette's map (1673) under the name of Ouemessourit, probably a corruption of their name by the Illinois tribe, with the characteristic Algonquian prefix. The name Missouri was first used by Joutel in 1687. In 1723 Bourgmont located their principal village 30 leagues below Kaw river and 60 leagues below the chief settlement of the Kansa; according to Croghan, they were located on Mississippi river opposite the Illinois country in 1759. Although the early locations are somewhat indefinite, it seems certain that the tribe formerly dwelt on the Mississippi about the mouth of the Missouri, and that they gradually ascended the latter stream, remaining for a time between Grand and Chariton rivers and establishing a town on the left bank of the Missouri near the mouth of the Grand. There they were found by French traders, who built a fort on an island quite near their village about the beginning of the eighteenth century. Soon afterward they were conquered and dispersed by a combination of Sac, Fox, and other Indians; they also suffered from smallpox. On the division, five or six lodges joined the Osage, two or three took refuge with the Kansa, and most of the remainder amalgamated with the Oto. In 1805 Lewis and Clark found a part of the tribe, numbering about 300, south of Platte river. The only known survivors in 1829 were with the Oto, when they numbered no more than 80. In 1842 their village stood on the southern bank of Platte river near the Oto settlement, and they followed the latter tribe to Indian Territory in 1882.

According to Winnebago tradition, the Loiwe're tribes separated from that "People of the parent speech" long ago, the Iowa being the first and the Oto the last to leave. In 1673 the Oto were located by Marquette west of Missouri river, between the fortieth and fortyfirst parallels; in 1680 they were 130 leagues from the Illinois, almost opposite the mouth of the Miskonsing (Wisconsin), and in 1687 they were on Osage river. According to La Hontan they were, in 1690, on Otontas (Osage) river; and in 1698 Hennepin placed them ten days' journey from Fort Crève Cœur. Iberville, in 1700, located the Iowa and Oto with the Omaha, between Wisconsin and Missouri rivers, about 100 leagues from the Illinois tribe; and Charlevoix, in 1721, fixed the Oto habitat as below that of the Iowa and above that of the Kansa on the western side of the Missouri. Dupratz mentions the Oto as a small nation on Missouri river in 1758, and Jefferys (1761) described them as occupying the southern bank of the Panis (Platte) between its mouth and the Pawnee territory; according to Porter, they occupied the same position in 1829. The Oto claimed the land bordering the Platte from their village to the mouth of the river, and also that on both sides of the Missouri as far as the Big Nemaha. In 1833 Catlin found the Oto and Missouri together in the Pawnee country; about 1841 they were gathered in four villages on the southern side of the Platte, from 5 to 18 miles above its mouth. In 1880 a part of the tribe removed to the Sac and Fox reservation in Indian Territory, where they still remain; in 1882 the rest of the tribe, with the remnant of the Missouri, emigrated to the Ponka, Pawnee, and Oto reservation in the present Oklahoma, where, in 1890 they were found to number 400.

WINNEBAGO

Linguistically the Winnebago Indians are closely related to the Loiwe're on the one side and to the Mandan on the other. They were first mentioned in the Jesuit Relation of 1636, though the earliest known use of the name Winnebago occurs in the Relation of 1640; Nicollet found them on Green bay in 1639. According to Shea, the Winnebago were almost annihilated by the Illinois (Algonquian) tribe in early days, and the historical group was made up of the survivors of the early battles. Chauvignerie placed the Winnebago on Lake Superior in 1736, and Jefferys referred to them and the Sac as living near the head of Green bay in 1764; Carver mentions a Winnebago village on a small island near the eastern end of Winnebago lake in 1778. Pike enumerated seven Winnebago villages existing in 1811; and in 1822 the population of the tribe was estimated at 5,800 including 900 warriors, in the country about Winnebago lake and extending thence southwestward to the Mississippi. By treaties in 1825 and 1832 they ceded their lands south of Wisconsin and Fox rivers for a reservation on the Mississippi above the Oneota; one of their villages in 1832 was at Prairie la Crosse. They suffered several visitations of smallpox; the third, which occurred in 1836, carried off more than a quarter of the tribe. A part of the people long remained widely distributed over their old country east of the Mississippi and along that river in Iowa and Minnesota; in 1840 most of the tribe removed to the neutral ground in the then territory of Iowa; in 1846 they surrendered their reservation for another above the Minnesota, and in 1856 they were removed to Blue Earth, Minnesota. Here they were mastering agriculture, when the Sioux war broke out and the settlers demanded their removal. Those who had taken up farms, thereby abandoning tribal rights, were allowed to remain, but the others were transferred to Crow creek, on Missouri river, whence they soon escaped. Their privations and sufferings were terrible; out of 2,000 taken to Crow creek only 1,200 reached the Omaha reservation, whither most of them fled. They were assigned a new reservation on the Omaha lands, where they now remain, occupying lands allotted in severalty. In 1890 there were 1,215 Winnebago on the reservation, but nearly an equal number were scattered over Minnesota, Iowa, Wisconsin, and Michigan, where they now live chiefly by agriculture, with a strong predilection for hunting.

MANDAN

The Mandan had a vague tradition of emigration from the eastern part of the country, and Lewis and Clark, Prince Maximilian, and others found traces of Mandan house-structures at various points along the Missouri; thus they appear to have ascended that stream before the advent of the Ǫegiha. During the historical period their movements were limited; they were first visited in the upper Missouri country by Sieur de la Verendrye in 1738. About 1750 they established two villages on the eastern side and seven on the western side of the Missouri, near the mouth of Heart river. Here they were assailed by the Asiniboin and Dakota and attacked by smallpox, and were greatly reduced; the two eastern villages consolidated, and the people migrated up the Missouri to a point 1,430 miles above its mouth (as subsequently determined by Lewis and Clark ; the seven villages were soon reduced to five, and these people also ascended the river and formed two villages in the Arikara country, near the Mandan of the eastern side, where they remained until about 1766, when they also consolidated. Thus the once powerful and populous tribe was reduced to two villages which, in 1804, were found by Lewis and Clark on opposite banks of the Missouri, about 4 miles below Knife river. Here for a time the tribe waxed and promised to regain the early prestige, reaching a population of 1,600 in 1837; but in that year they were again attacked by smallpox and almost annihilated, the survivors numbering only 31 according to one account, or 125 to 145 according to others. After this visitation they united in one village. When the Hidatsa removed from Knife river in 1845, some of the Mandan accompanied them, and others followed at intervals as late as 1858, when only a few still remained at their old home. In 1872 a reservation was set apart for the Hidatsa and Arikara and the survivors of the Mandan on Missouri and Yellowstone rivers in Dakota and Montana, but in 1886 the reservation was reduced. According to the census returns, the Mandan numbered 252 in 1890.

HIDATSA

There has been much confusion concerning the definition and designation of the Hidatsa Indians. They were formerly known as Minitari or Gros Ventres of the Missouri, in distinction from the Gros Ventres of the plains, who belong to another stock. The origin of the term Gros Ventres is somewhat obscure, and various observers have pointed out its inapplicability, especially to the well-formed Hidatsa tribesmen. According to Dorsey, the French pioneers probably translated a native term referring to a traditional buffalo paunch, which occupies a prominent place in the Hidatsa mythology and which, in early times, led to a dispute and the separation of the Crow from the main group some time in the eighteenth century.

The earlier legends of the Hidatsa are vague, but there is a definite tradition of a migration northward, about 1765, from the neighborhood of Heart river, where they were associated with the Mandan, to Knife river. At least as early as 1796, according to Matthews, there were three villages belonging to this tribe on Knife river—one at the mouth, another half a mile above, and the third and largest 3 miles from the mouth. Here the people were found by Lewis and Clark in 1804, and here they remained until 1837, when the scourge of smallpox fell and many of the people perished, the survivors uniting in a single village. About 1845 the Hidatsa and a part of the Mandan again migrated up the Missouri, and established a village 30 miles by land and 60 miles by water above their old home, within what is now Fort Berthold reservation. Their population has apparently varied greatly, partly by reason of the ill definition of the tribe by different enumerators, partly by reason of the inroads of smallpox. In 1890 they numbered 522.

The Crow people are known by the Hidatsa as Kihatsa They-refused-the-paunch , according to Matthews; and Dorsey points out that their own name, Absaruke, does not mean "crow," but refers to a variety of hawk. Lewis and Clark found the tribe in four bands. In 1817 Brown located them on Yellowstone river. In 1829 they were described by Porter as ranging along Yellowstone river on the eastern side of the Rocky mountains, and numbered at 4,000; while in 1834, according to Drake, they occupied the southern branch of the Yellowstone, about the fortysixth parallel and one hundred and fifth meridian, with a population of 4,500. In 1842 their number was estimated at 4,000, and they were described as inhabiting the headwaters of the Yellowstone. They have since been duly gathered on the Crow reservation in Montana, and are slowly adopting civilization. In 1890 they numbered 2,287.

THE EASTERN AND SOUTHERN TRIBES

The history of the Monakan, Catawba, Sara, Pedee, and Santee, and incidentally that of the Biloxi, has been carefully reviewed in a recent publication by Mooney,[1] and does not require repetition.

GENERAL MOVEMENTS

On reviewing the records of explorers and pioneers and the few traditions which have been preserved, the course of Siouan migration and development becomes clear. In general the movements were westward and northwestward. The Dakota tribes have not been traced far, though several of them, like the Yanktonnai, migrated hundreds of miles from the period of first observation to the end of the eighteenth century; then came the Mandan, according to their tradition, and as they ascended the Missouri left traces of their occupancy scattered over 1,000 miles of migration; next the Çegiha descended the Ohio and passed from the cis-Mississippi forests over the trans-Mississippi plains—the stronger branch following the Mandan, while the lesser at first descended the great river and then worked up the Arkansas into the buffalo country until checked and diverted by antagonistic tribes. So also the Ḳoiwe're, first recorded near the Mississippi, pushed 300 miles westward; while the Winnebago gradually emigrated from the region of the Great Lakes into the trans-Mississippi country even before their movements were affected by contact with white men. In like manner the Hidatsa are known to have flowed northwestward many scores of miles; and the Asiniboin swept more rapidly across the plains from the place of their rebellion against the Yanktonnai, on the Mississippi, before they found final resting place on the Saskatchewan

[1] Siouan Tribes of the East, 1894.

plains 500 or 800 miles away. All of the movements were consistent and, despite intertribal friction and strife, measurably harmonious. The lines of movement, so far as they can be restored, are in full accord with the lines of linguistic evolution traced by Hale and Dorsey and Gatschet, and indicate that some five hundred or possibly one thousand years ago the tribesmen pushed over the Appalachians to the Ohio and followed that stream and its tributaries to the Mississippi (though there are faint indications that some of the early emigrants ascended the northern tributaries to the region of the Great Lakes); and that the human flood gained volume as it advanced and expanded to cover the entire region of the plains. The records concerning the movement of this great human stream find support in the manifest reason for the movement; the reason was the food quest by which all primitive men are led, and its end was the abundant fauna of the prairieland, with the buffalo at its head.

While the early population of the Siouan stock, when first the huntsmen crossed the Appalachians, may not be known, the lines of migration indicate that the people increased and multiplied amain during their long journey, and that their numbers culminated, despite external conflict and internal strife, about the beginning of written history, when the Siouan population may have been 100,000 or more. Then came war against the whites and the still more deadly smallpox, whereby the vigorous stock was checked and crippled and the population gradually reduced; but since the first shock, which occurred at different dates in different parts of the great region, the Siouan people have fairly held their own, and some branches are perhaps gaining in strength.

SOME FEATURES OF INDIAN SOCIOLOGY

As shown by Powell, there are two fundamentally distinct classes or stages in human society—(1) tribal society and (2) national society. National society characterizes civilization; primarily it is organized on a territorial basis, but as enlightenment grows the bases are multiplied. Tribal society is characteristic of savagery and barbarism; so far as known, all tribal societies are organized on the basis of kinship. The transfer from tribal society to national society is often, perhaps always, through feudalism, in which the territorial motive takes root and in which the kinship motive withers.

All of the American aborigines north of Mexico and most of those farther southward were in the stage of tribal society when the continents were discovered, though feudalism was apparently budding in South America, Central America, and parts of Mexico. The partly developed transitional stage may, for the present, be neglected, and American Indian sociology may be considered as representing tribal society or kinship organization.

The fundamental principles of tribal organization through kinship have been formulated by Powell; they are as follows:[1]

I. A body of kindred constituting a distinct body politic is divided into groups, the males into groups of brothers and the females into groups of sisters, on distinctions of generations, regardless of degrees of consanguinity; and the kinship terms used express relative age. In civilized society kinships are classified on distinctions of sex, distinctions of generations, and distinctions arising from degrees of consanguinity.

II. When descent is in the female line, the brother-group consists of natal brothers, together with all the materterate male cousins of whatever degree. Thus mother's sisters' sons and mother's mother's sisters' daughters' sons, etc, are included in a group with natal brothers. In like manner the sister-group is composed of natal sisters, together with all materterate female cousins of whatever degree.

III. When descent is in the male line, the brother-group is composed of natal brothers, together with all patruate male cousins of whatever degree, and the sister-group is composed of natal sisters, together with all patruate female cousins of whatever degree.

IV. The son of a member of a brother-group calls each one of the group, father; the father of a member of a brother-group calls each one of the group, son. Thus a father-group is coextensive with the brother-group to which the father belongs. A brother-group may also constitute a father-group and grandfather-group, a son-group and a grandson-group. It may also be a patruate-group and an avunculate-group. It may also be a patruate cousin-group and an avunculate cousin-group; and in general, every member of a brother-group has the same consanguineal relation to persons outside of the group as that of every other member.

Two postulates concerning primitive society, adopted by various ethnologic students of other countries, have been erroneously applied to the American aborigines; at the same time they have been so widely accepted as to demand consideration.

The first postulate is that primitive men were originally assembled in chaotic hordes, and that organized society was developed out of the chaotic mass by the segregation of groups and the differentiation of functions within each group. Now the American aborigines collectively represent a wide range in development, extending from a condition about as primitive as ever observed well toward the verge of feudalism, and thus offer opportunities for testing the postulate; and it has been found that when higher and lower stages representing any portion of the developmental succession are compared, the social organizations of the lower grade are no less definite, perhaps more definite, than those pertaining to the higher grade; so that when the history of demotic growth among the American Indians is traced backward, the organizations are found on the whole to grow more definite, albeit more simple. When the lines of development revealed through research are projected still farther toward their origin, they indicate an initial condition, directly antithetic to the postulated horde, in which the scant population was segregated in small discrete bodies, probably family groups; and that in each of these bodies there was a definite organization, while each group was practically independent of, and probably

[1] Third Annual Report of the Bureau of Ethnology, for 1881–82 (1884), pp. xliv–xlv.

inimical to. all other groups. The testimony of the observed institutions is corroborated by the testimony of language, which, as clearly shown by Powell,[1] represents progressive combination rather than continued differentiation, a process of involution rather than evolution. It would appear that the original definitely organized groups occasionally met and coalesced, whereby changes in organization were required; that these compound groups occasionally coalesced with other groups, both simple and compound, whereby they were elaborated in structure, always with some loss in definiteness and permanence; and that gradually the groups enlarged by incorporation, while the composite organization grew complex and variable to meet the ever-changing conditions. It would also appear that in some cases the corporeal growth outran the structural or institutional growth, when the bodies—clans, gentes, tribes, or confederacies—split into two or more fragments which continued to grow independently; yet that in general the progress of institutional development went forward through incorporation of peoples and differentiation of institutions. The same process was followed as tribal society passed into national society; and it is the same process which is today exalting national society into world society, and transforming simple civilization into enlightenment. Thus the evolution of social organization is from the simple and definite toward the complex and variable: or from the involuntary to the voluntary; or from the environment-shaped to the environment-shaping; or from the biotic to the demotic.

The second postulate, which may be regarded as a corollary of the first, is that the primary conjugal condition was one of promiscuity, out of which different forms of marriage were successively segregated. Now the wide range in institutional development exemplified by the American Indians affords unprecedented opportunities for testing this postulate also. The simplest demotic unit found among the aborigines is the clan or mother-descent group, in which the normal conjugal relation is essentially monogamous,[2] in which marriage is more or less strictly regulated by a system of prohibitions, and in which the chief conjugal regulation is commonly that of exogamy with respect to the clan: in higher groups, more deeply affected by contact with neighboring peoples, the simple clan organization is sometimes found to be modified, (1) by the adoption and subsequent conjugation of captive men and boys, and, doubtless more profoundly, (2) by the adoption and polygamous marriage of female captives; and in still more highly organized groups the mother-descent is lost and polygamy is regular and limited only by the capacity of the husband as a provider. The second and third stages are commonly characterized, like the first,

[1] Notably in "Relation of primitive peoples to environment, illustrated by American examples," Smithsonian Report for 1896, pp. 625-638, especially p. 635.

[2] Neither space nor present occasion warrants discussion of the curious aphrodisian cults found among many peoples, usually in the barbaric stage of development; it may be noted merely that this is an aberrant branch from the main stem of institutional growth. The subject is touched briefly in "The beginning of marriage," American Anthropologist, vol. IX, pp. 371-383, Nov., 1896.

by established prohibitions and by clan exogamy; though with the
advance in organization amicable relations with certain other groups
are usually established, whereby the germ of tribal organization is
implanted and a system of interclan marriage, or tribal endogamy, is
developed.   With further advance the mother descent group is transformed into a father-descent group, when the clan is replaced by the
gens; and polygamy is a common feature of the gentile organization,
In all of these stages the conjugal and consanguineal regulations are
affected by the militant habits characteristic of primitive groups; more
warriors than women are slain in battle, and there are more female
captives than male; and thus the polygamy is mainly or wholly
polygyny.   In many cases civil conditions combine with or partially
replace the militant conditions, yet the tendency of conjugal development is not changed.   Among the Seri Indians, probably the most
primitive tribe in North America, in which the demotic unit is the
clan, there is a rigorous marriage custom under which the would-be
groom is required to enter the family of the girl and demonstrate (1)
his capacity as a provider and (2) his strength of character as a man,
by a year's probation, before he is finally accepted—the conjugal the-
ory of the tribe being monogamy, though the practice, at least during
recent years, has, by reason of conditions, passed into polygyny.
Among several other tribes of more provident and less exclusive habit,
the first of the two conditions recognized by the Seri is met by rich
presents (representing accumulated property) from the groom to the
girl's family, the second condition being usually ignored, the clan
organization remaining in force; among still other tribes the first condition is more or less vaguely recognized, though the voluntary present
is commuted into, or replaced by, a negotiated value exacted by the
girl's family, when the mother descent is commonly vestigial; and in
the next stage, which is abundantly exemplified, wife-purchase pre-
vails, and the clan is replaced by the gens.   In this succession the
development of wife-purchase and the decadence of mother-descent
may be traced, and it is significant that there is a tendency first toward
partial enslavement of the wife and later toward the multiplication of
wives to the limit of the husband's means, and toward transforming
all, or all but one, of the wives into menials.   Thus the lines of development under militant and civil conditions are essentially parallel.   It
is possible to project these lines some distance backward into the
unknown of the exceedingly primitive, when they are found to define
small discrete bodies—just such as are indicated by the institutional
and linguistic lines—probably family groups, which must have been
essentially, and were perhaps strictly, monogamous.   It would appear
that in these groups mating was either between distant members
(under a law of attraction toward the remote and repulsion from the
near, which is shared by mankind and the higher animals), or the result
of accidental meeting between nubile members of different groups;
that in the second case and sometimes in the first the conjugation

produced a new monogamic family; and that sometimes in the first case (and possibly in the second) the new group retained a more or less definite connection with the parent group—this connection constituting the germ of the clan. In passing, it may be noted merely that this inferential origin of the lines of institutional development is in accord with the habits of certain higher and incipiently organized animals. From this hypothetic beginning, primitive marriage may be traced through the various observed stages of monogamy and polygamy and concubinage and wife-subordination, through savagery and barbarism and into civilization, with its curious combination of exoteric monogamy and esoteric promiscuity. Fortunately the burden of the proof of this evolution does not now rest wholly on the evidence obtained among the American aborigines; for Westermarck has recently reviewed the records of observation among the primitive peoples of many lands, and has found traces of the same sequence in all.[1] Thus the evolution of marriage, like that of other human institutions, is from the simple and definite to the complex and variable; i. e., from approximate or complete monogamy through polygamy to a mixed status of undetermined signification: or from the mechanical to the spontaneous: or from the involuntary to the voluntary; or from the provincial to the cosmopolitan.

As implied in several foregoing paragraphs, and as clearly set forth in various publications by Powell, tribal society falls into two classes or stages—(1) clan organization and (2) gentile organization, these stages corresponding respectively to savagery and barbarism, strictly defined.

At the time of discovery, most of the American Indians were in the upper stages of savagery and the lower stages of barbarism, as defined by organization; among some tribes descent was reckoned in the female line, though definite matriarchies have not been discovered; among several tribes descent was and still is reckoned in the male line, and among all of the tribes thus far investigated the patriarchal system is found.

In tribal society, both clan and gentile, the entire social structure is based on real or assumed kinship, and a large part of the demotic devices are designed to establish, perpetuate, and advertise kinship relations. As already indicated, the conspicuous devices in order of development are the taboo with the prohibitions growing out of it, kinship nomenclature and regulations, and a system of ordination by which incongruous things are brought into association.

Among the American Indians the taboo and derivative prohibitions are used chiefly in connection with marriage and clan or gentile organization. Marriage in the clan or gens is prohibited; among many tribes a vestige of the inferential primitive condition is found in the curious

---

[1] The History of Human Marriage (London, 1891), especially chapters iv–vi, xiii–xv, xx–xxii.

prohibition of communications between children-in-law and parents-in-law; the clan taboos are commonly connected with the tutelar beast-god, perhaps represented by a totem.

The essential feature of the kinship terminology is the reckoning from ego, whereby each individual remembers his own relation to every other member of the clan or tribe; and commonly the kinship terms are classific rather than descriptive (i. e., a single term expresses the relation which in English is expressed by the phrase "My elder brother's second son's wife"). The system is curiously complex and elaborate. It was not discovered by the earlier and more superficial observers of the Indians, and was brought out chiefly by Morgan, who detected numerous striking examples among different tribes; but it would appear that the system is not equally complete among all of the tribes, probably because of immature development in some cases and because of decadence in others.

The system of ordination, like that of kinship, is characterized by reckoning from the ego and by adventitious associations. It may have been developed from the kinship system through the need for recognition and assignment of adopted captives, collective property, and other things pertaining to the group; yet it bears traces of influence by the taboo system. Its ramifications are wide: In some cases it emphasizes kinship by assigning members of the family group to fixed positions about the camp-fire or in the house; this function develops into the placement of family groups in fixed order, as exemplified in the Iroquoian long-house and the Siouan camping circle; or it develops into a curiously exaggerated direction concept culminating in the cult of the Four Quarters and the Here, and this prepares the way for a quinary, decimal, and vigesimal numeration; this last branch sends off another in which the cult of the Six Quarters and the Here arises to prepare the way for the mystical numbers 7, 13, and 7×7, whose vestiges come down to civilization; both the four-quarter and the six-quarter associations are sometimes bound up with colors; and there are numberless other ramifications. Sometimes the function and development of these curious concepts, which constitute perhaps the most striking characteristic of prescriptorial culture, are obscure at first glance, and hardly to be discovered even through prolonged research; yet, so far as they have been detected and interpreted, they are especially adapted to fixing demotic relations; and through them the manifold relations of individuals and groups are crystallized and kept in mind.

Thus the American Indians, including the Siouan stock, are made up of families organized into clans or gentes, and combined in tribes, sometimes united in confederacies, all on a basis of kinship, real or assumed; and the organization is shaped and perpetuated by a series of devices pertaining to the plane of prescriptorial culture, whereby each member of the organization is constantly reminded of his position in the group.